Guiding the Human Resources Function in Education

Guiding the Human Resources Function in Education

New Issues, New Needs

M. Scott Norton

ROWMAN & LITTLEFIELD
Lanham • Boulder • New York • London

Published by Rowman & Littlefield
A wholly owned subsidiary of The Rowman & Littlefield Publishing Group, Inc.
4501 Forbes Boulevard, Suite 200, Lanham, Maryland 20706
www.rowman.com

Unit A, Whitacre Mews, 26–34 Stannary Street, London SE11 4AB

British Library Cataloguing in Publication Information Available

Library of Congress Cataloging-in-Publication Data Is Available

ISBN 978-1-4758-2977-8 (cloth : alk. paper)
ISBN 978-1-4758-2978-5 (paper : alk. paper)
ISBN 978-1-4758-2979-2 (electronic)

♾️™ The paper used in this publication meets the minimum requirements of American National Standard for Information Sciences—Permanence of Paper for Printed Library Materials, ANSI/NISO Z39.48–1992.

Printed in the United States of America

Contents

Preface

WHY THE BOOK WAS WRITTEN

The primary focus of the book is to emphasize the major changes in the leadership responsibilities of directors of human resources in education. This purpose underscores the necessity for HR directors to gain new knowledge and skills in order to assure that the personnel concept is considered in all school district policy and administrative program decisions. The primary processes of the human resources function remain significant, but the function's importance is continually increasing as new and innovative changes are evidenced in education.

Personnel recruitment, for example, now necessitates important attention to re-recruitment. Innovation in mentoring activities now includes reverse mentoring, peer mentoring, and group mentoring. Metrics now loom important and necessary in program planning, accountability, and assessment activities. The knowledge and skills required for new innovations were not always available in the preparation programs of personnel who focused on preparation for general school administration. This book will help practicing human resources directors and others who will enter the personnel field to understand and meet the demands of today's human resources needs by

- identifying and describing the ever-changing issues, problems, challenges, and trends being encountered in the human resources function today;
- introducing and discussing many new and innovative changes being introduced into the human resources function;
- recommending and describing changes that must be made in the human resources director's position in order to meet the new requirements of the job;

- examining the benefits of coaching and mentoring services with attention given to the innovative strategies related to these services;
- presenting best practices by discussing empirical and basic research findings relative to the human factors of job satisfaction, motivation, and achievement;
- discussing recommendations for necessary changes in the programs of administrator preparation for the position of human resources director;
- giving due importance to the work of classified personnel in relation to their importance in meeting the stated purposes of the school district's educational program purposes.

Introduction

HOW THE BOOK IS ORGANIZED

The primary themes of the book serve to (1) underscore the increasing importance of the human resources function in education and set forth the changing design and analysis for the position of director of the program, (2) demonstrate the vital importance of planning and organizational development for effective human resources allocation and for integrating the human resources planning into the school district's strategic program plan, (3) establish guidelines for implementing new and innovative primary human resources processes that increase program effectiveness, (4) re-enforce the vital importance of focusing on personnel management toward the maximization of the organization's administration potential, and (5) emphasize the comprehensiveness of the responsibilities of the human resources director and the importance of upgrading the position administratively relative to program decisions within the school district.

Chapter 1 of the book centers on the topic of the human resources director and the need to update the position's analysis and design. Chapter 2 sets forth the essentials of re-assessing the process of human resources planning and organization. Effectively staffing the schools for educational and support services is the focus of chapter 3. Chapter 4 centers on the human resources purpose of the maximization of human potential, and chapter 5 underscores the working world of the school district's classified personnel and their direct relationship to the achievement of school district goals and objectives.

The book is viewed as a core text that serves as an effective supplement for many different college and in-service programs and courses on the general topic of organizational development and administrative management. Professors who teach courses in administration that center on the school

principalship, administrative leadership, supervision, the school superintendency, and school personnel will find the book to be of special value. Practicing school administrators should have a copy of the book in their professional
libraries for use as a guide in the implementation of personnel practices and
policy decisions.

Each chapter of the book opens with a statement of primary purpose.
Reader engagement is enhanced by having readers participate in quizzes specifically designed as learning experiences. Chapter snapshots, best program
practices, discussion questions, case studies, and references for extended
learning are included in each chapter. A summary of best ideas and recommendations is set forth at the close of each chapter.

Many new personnel topics and strategies are presented in the book,
including metrics for program evaluation and assessment. Innovative strategies such as reverse and group mentoring are discussed and principles of
adult learning are set forth in relation to improving staff development activities. Examples of effective human resources models for position analysis
and other strategic practices that enhance the effectiveness of the human
resources function will engage the readers and motivate them to implement
new innovations in their current work.

Chapter 1

Meeting the Challenges in Human Resources Administration

Primary chapter goal: To underscore the primary importance of the human resources function in educational administration and set forth the changing design and analysis for the position of director of human resources.

HUMAN RESOURCES POSITION DESIGN AND ANALYSIS

The first book that focused on the function of personnel in organizations was *Personnel Administration*, authored by Tead and Metcalf in 1920. The book established the principles and the best prevailing practices in the field of administration and human relations in industry. As these authors stated nearly 100 years ago

> personnel administration is the direction and coordination of the human relations of any organization with a view to getting the maximum necessary production with a minimum of effort and friction, and with proper regard for the genuine well-being of the worker. . ... The new focus in administration is to be the human element. The new center of attention and solicitude is the individual person, the worker. . . Present development is in the direction of a newly appreciated art— the science and art of personnel administration. (pp. 1–2)

Contemporary definitions of the personnel function in education, such as the one that follows, tend to reflect similar purposes: "The human resources function [comprises] those processes that are planned and implemented in the school system to establish an effective system of human resources and

1

to foster an organizational climate that enhances the accomplishment of the system's educational mission, fosters the personal and professional objectives of the employees, and engages the support of the school community in which the school system is embedded" (Norton, 2008, p. 409).

Historically, the guiding purposes of realizing maximum production, caring for the well-being of the workers, implementing an effective system of human resources (HR), fostering a positive organizational climate, focusing on the human element, maximizing employee satisfaction, doing what's best for teachers, accomplishing educational goals, gaining the support of the school community, maximizing employee performance, and demonstrating concern for the management of people have founded personnel practices in all organizations.

This chapter focuses on the recommended responsibilities of the position of human resources director in education, including the increasing importance of change management and workforce diversity. Other chapters focus on workforce planning, the continuing importance of effective recruitment and selection of personnel, strategies for assuring continuous personnel growth and development, the importance of performance, financial and compensation administration, the supportive work of classified personnel, and other important administrative processes of the human resources function in education.

For 2017 and the near future, the focus on the HR function gives special attention to change management, retention of talent, diversity in the workplace, funding, personnel compensation, career development, human relations, administrative openness, and the fact that public schools are facing increasing "competition" from charter schools and other private school movements.

We ask that you take a few minutes to complete the following pre-quiz on the status and design of the human resource administrator's position in education. Answer each of the true or false statements and then check your responses with the answers at the end of the quiz. It's OK to make a good guess in answering the question, but just don't "wing it." Rather, skip questions that you are really not certain about and move on to the next question.

PRE-QUIZ

One statewide study of the work of human resources directors found:

1. School human resources practitioners tend to agree that staffing the schools is the most important task they perform. _____True or _____False

2. Approximately three-fourths of the human resources directors were of the opinion that they were "well prepared" to assume the leadership role of human resources director. ____True or ____False

3. Only two position titles were reported for the persons leading the human resources unit: (i) director of human resources and (ii) administrator of personnel. ____True or ____False

4. Approximately two-thirds of the HR directors had served in their current position for four to five years. ____True or ____False

5. Approximately 90% of the directors had prior experience as a classroom teacher and 75% had prior experience as a school principal. ____True or ____ False.

6. 65% of the directors reported that human resources administration was a goal that they had had in mind during their graduate school program of preparation. ____True or ____False

7. Technical skills, conceptual skills, and human skills, in that rank order, were ranked by the study respondents relative to their importance for the work of HR director. ____True or ____False

8. The study participants believed that they were chosen for the HR director's role for the reason that "they were considered to be a highly effective classroom [teacher] or performed effectively in their role of school principal (or other educational position)." ____True or ____False

9. 71.5% of the human resources directors stated they "probably would not" assume the position of human resources director if starting over again professionally. ____True or ____False

10. When asked if the following statement came close to describing how they felt much of the time ("The problems of administering a school district's human resources program are all but insoluble; the life of the HR director is almost impossible. Sometimes I feel that I've had it. I'm just going to ride it out the best I can") two-thirds of the HR directors answered, "not close at all." ____True or ____False

11. A position analysis is synonymous with a position description. ____True or ____False

12. Although education will witness many societal changes in the next ten to twenty years, trends in HR administration indicate that this function will remain constant as a support and maintenance function. ____True or ____False

Answers to the Pre-Quiz

Question 1 is true, question 2 is false, question 3 is false, question 4 is false, question 5 is false, question 6 is false, question 7 is false, question 8 is false, question 9 is false, question 10 is true, question 11 is false, question 12 is false.

Scoring Results

Your Score

12–11 correct answers: You could "skip" chapter 1 and move on to chapter 2:
   Excellent work! *****
10–9 correct answers: A commendable performance: Nice work. ****
8–7 correct answers: A good effort. ***
6–5 correct answers: You'll enjoy the information in chapter 1.**
4–3 correct answers: Enjoy chapter 1. *
2–0 correct answers: Sorry, we are out of stars; you'll benefit by studying
   chapter 1.

Discussion of the Pre-Quiz

Question 1, "School human resources practitioners tend to agree that staffing
the schools is the most important task they perform," is true. In the aforementioned study, 82.9% of the human resources directors ranked the recruitment of personnel as their primary responsibility. "Recruitment can make or
break an organization because even a brilliant training module cannot repair
a faulty recruitment" (Public Administration, 2016, p. 4). The very objective
of a school's purpose, improving student academic achievement, depends on
the ability of the human resources department to recruit, select, and retain the
right talent.

The process of recruitment is discussed in later chapters of the book. Tied
to the process of recruitment is the processes of planning and organizing;
these processes are discussed in chapter 2. Without question, the loss of personnel, certificated and classified, is among the primary problems being faced
by HR directors today.

Question 2, "Approximately three-fourths of the human resources directors
were of the opinion that they were 'well prepared' to assume the leadership
role of human resources director," is false. Only one-fourth of the directors
was of the opinion that they were well prepared. About one-half of the directors judged themselves to be only "fairly well" prepared for the job. Only
10.7% had served in an assistant director's role prior to becoming a director,
and 10% had served in such a position in business or industry. It is clear that
degree programs in higher education must be greatly improved in regard to
preparing administrators in the area of human resources administration.

Question 3, "Only two position titles were reported for the persons leading
the human resources unit: (i) director of human resources and (ii) administrator of personnel," is false. Twenty-three different titles for such positions were reported. The titles of director of human resources, administrator
of personnel, human resources specialist, and assistant superintendent for

personnel services were among the many different titles. Most everyone uses and understands the titles of the school principal and superintendent of schools, but few can relate intelligently to the varying titles given to the administrator of the human resources function.

While the term *human resources* has replaced the term *personnel* in practice for the most part in organizations, even the national American Association of School Personnel Administrators retains the term *personnel* in its title. Consideration should be given to the assignment of position titles for the individual in charge of the personnel function. Both continuity and understanding of roles possibly might be enhanced by the implementation of some system of commonality in job descriptions and position titles.

Question 4, "Approximately two-thirds of the HR directors had served in their current position for four to five years," is false. In fact, only 25% of the directors had served in their present position for four to five years. Moreover, 42.6% of the directors had been in their present position for three years or less. Although this statistic might not be common for all states nationally, no director that participated in the study in question had twenty or more years in the role. Only 12.6% of the survey participants had served for more than ten years in the leadership role of human resources director.

Such information does not auger well for stability in the human resources director's position. Many factors impact on the administration of the human resources function in education. Change management, diverse workforce, inclusion, talent management, succession planning, employee relations, legal rulings, autonomy, talent retention strategies, budget cuts, technological advancements, recruitment challenges, accountability measures, state and federal mandates, and other factors bear heavily on the role and responsibilities of the human resources function. These factors and others are discussed in this and other chapters of the book.

Question 5, "Approximately 90% of the directors had prior experience as a classroom teacher and 75% had prior experience as a school principal," is false. The survey results revealed that 53.5% of the directors had prior experience as a classroom teacher, and approximately 40% had previously served as a school principal. Only 10.7% had served in an assistant HR director's role prior to becoming a director.

A slight majority of survey participants (53.5%) viewed prior experience as a teacher as being important or highly important for assuming the responsibilities of an HR director. A much higher percentage, 73.3%, viewed prior experience as an administrator as being important or highly important. Keep in mind that slightly less than one-third, 27.9%, of the survey participants had served previously in some position in business or industry.

Question 6, "65% of the directors reported that human resources administration was a goal that they had had in mind during their graduate school program of preparation," is false. In fact, only slightly more than one-fourth, 26.7%, reported that human resources administration was a goal that they had had in mind during their graduate school preparation program.

Question 7, "Technical skills, conceptual skills, and human skills, in that rank order, were ranked by the study respondents relative to their importance for the work of HR director," is false.

Human skills, by a landslide, ranked as the most important skill for the HR director's effectiveness in the role. Many skills are required for effective performance in the HR administrator's position; most of them can be classified under the human, conceptual, and technical headlines.

Question 8, "The study participants believed that they were chosen for the HR director's role for the reason that 'they were considered to be a highly effective classroom [teacher] or performed effectively in their role of school principal (or other educational position),' " is false. We reasonably could assume that these factors were considered in the HR director's appointment to the position, but the directors themselves reported that they believed they were selected for the role due to the fact they were identified as being highly effective in human relations and were identified as one that could achieve needed improvements in the HR function.

Question 9, "71.5% of the human resources directors stated they 'probably would not' assume the position of human resources director if starting over again professionally," is false. Only 9.1% of the survey participants indicated that "they probably would not assume the position of human resources director if starting over again."

Question 10, "When asked if the following statement came close to describing how they felt much of the time [HR director's position was impossible], two-thirds of the HR directors answered, 'not close at all,' " is true. However, one-third indicated that the statement was "very close" or was "close" to their position on the matter.

In spite of high levels of job pressure and stress, the large majority of HR directors were enjoying their work, and job satisfaction levels were very high or high. In fact, nearly 90% of the survey participants reported that they enjoyed the position "most all" of the time. Leading troublesome issues included the demands of the position itself, problems related to teacher personnel, external demands and requirements from state and federal agencies, and the demands/problems related to classified personnel. The number one issue that would lead one to leaving the position would be the development of an unsatisfactory working relationship with the school superintendent or another supervisor.

Question 11, "A position analysis is synonymous with a position description," is false. A position description is based on the information derived from a position analysis. A *position analysis* is a scientific, comprehensive analysis of a job that includes its constituent parts and its internal and external conditions. A *position description* commonly includes the job title, major duties, evaluation responsibilities, coordination activities, position qualifications, and the supervision given and received. Among its many uses is serving as a basis for recruiting and interviewing applicants for school positions and clarifying employee responsibilities and specific duties.

Question 12, "Although education will witness many societal changes in the next ten to twenty years, trends in HR administration indicate that this function will remain constant as a support and maintenance function," is false. As noted by Young (2008), "the human resources function plays a vital role in helping the system operate within the economic structures, meet legal mandates, honor contractual obligations, address pressures of special interest groups, adapt to emerging technologies, and uphold ethical standards while maintaining centrality of purpose" (p. 1).

BASIC SKILLS FOR HUMAN EFFECTIVENESS

Table 1.1 shows the results of the survey relative to the participants' perceptions of personnel skills of most importance in their present position of HR director. Human skills center on one's ability to function effectively with a diverse workforce. Conceptual skills are revealed in one's ability to use data/information to analyze and resolve problems that are encountered in the organization's operations. Technical skills center on one's knowledge and aptitude to plan, organize, and implement the purposes of the organization.

The rankings of necessary skills do change with always evolving social, economic, and political conditions and demands. Human relations skills, including the characteristic of *trust*, loom as highly significant for HR directors. The rather low ranking of research skill, noted in Table 1.1, will become a greater need in future practice. General management skills tie closely to *system efficiency*. Keeping system analysis and the concept of system fully

Table 1.1. Necessary Skills for Human Resources Effectiveness

Necessary Skills	Rank	Percentage Response
Human Relations Skill	1	85.4
Legal Skill	2	48.0
General Management Skill	3–4	39.0
Communication Skill	3–4	39.0
Political Skill	5	31.7
Conflict Management Skill	6	29.3
Negotiation Skill	7	14.6
Research Skill	8	7.3

in mind, payroll and cooperative administration/staff relations are among the primary issues/needs that are discussed in later chapters of the book.

Of course, many other related skills are important in the work of the HR director, including effectiveness skills, observation skills, monitor-performance skills, professional development skills, and decision-making skills. Early researchers, such as Follett, Mayo, Herzberg, Mausner and Snyderman, McGregor, and Likert, made foundational contributions to human resources and contemporary practices of human relations.

Mary Parker Follett (1924) spoke of "power with" rather than "power over" members of the organization. The concern of management should be the building and maintenance of dynamic yet harmonious relationships. Herzberg, Mausner, and Snyderman (1959) underscored the difference between factors that lead to job satisfaction and those that lead to job dissatisfaction. While achievement tends to bring about job motivation and job satisfaction, the absence of this factor does not necessarily result in job dissatisfaction. The factors of job dissatisfaction are evident in bad company policy and administration, poor methods of supervision, inadequate salary, and poor working conditions.

Douglass McGregor's Theory Y (1960) opened new doors to thinking about leadership styles and human potential in organizations. Rensis Likert (1967) viewed people as an investment as opposed to an expense, and he developed a model for measuring these human assets. Likert's linking pin concept of horizontal and vertical communication was revolutionary. His Likert-type assessment scales are prominent today in human resources surveys used by school districts to assess public opinions relative to the accomplishment of the school's program.

EMERGING TRENDS AND THE HUMAN RESOURCES FUNCTION

Some organizational leaders have referred to the trends taking place in human resources nationally as being *revolutionary*; others have used the term *evolutionary*. Whether the changes in the human resources function are viewed as major fundamental changes or as the continuous redesigning of the HR function's processes, the function in educational settings is witnessing major forces that impact the workplace, the workforce, the worker, and the work itself (Deloitte, 2016).

The literature speaks of global trends, emerging trends, political trends, economic trends, social trends, technological trends, and other "happenings" taking place that influence practices in the human resources function. Human resources *trends* such as globalization; new technologies; competition or organizational changes, including multicultural diversity; retaining talent; leadership development; and transformations in the human resources function, epitomized by talent management, work flexibility, and accountability, have major implications for the important responsibilities of the human resources leader in school districts nationally.

We read of the war for talent, work-life balance, capital trends, succession planning, labor relations, mergers and acquisitions, human resources management, reverse mentoring, increased accountability, and technological innovations. Workforce diversity is important as well. Important considerations within workforce diversity include gender, race, age, social class, sexual orientation, values, personality, character, ethnicity, religion, education, language, physical appearance, marital status, lifestyle, beliefs, ideologies, and background characteristics such as geographic origin and economic status.

POSITION ANALYSIS: A FORGOTTEN VITAL TOOL FOR HUMAN RESOURCES PLANNING

Who benefits by the completion of a job analysis? The answer is most everyone. Why isn't the completion of job analyses more popular and commonly practiced in education? The answers rest in the facts that the process is overlooked in most every administrator preparation program, few HR directors appear to be knowledgeable of the steps needed for completing a job analysis, and the process itself is somewhat complex, time-consuming, and costly. Given its importance and benefits for the school district's administration, teaching personnel and classified personnel lend important positive outcomes for the entire school relationships that exist between the individual employee and his or her immediate supervisor.

An effective job analysis can be of value to the school district and to the employees of the school district. A job analysis serves the school district in determining the best methods for implementing a position under the internal and external conditions in which it exists. Such information facilitates the planning, scheduling, resourcing, and evaluating the operations of the position. Improvement of the operations of a job necessitates knowledge of the foregoing processes.

Defining the job's specifications facilitates the implementation of standards to be achieved, the training that is necessary, and other affective and cognitive characteristics required for achieving the primary outcomes desired by the work of the position. Knowing the effects of the job on the worker is necessary for reducing worker turnover and fostering worker cooperation. In addition, effective job analyses will enable the school district to coordinate jobs more effectively and promote more cordial working relationships between and among school district offices and local school operations.

BENEFITS TO THE SCHOOL EMPLOYEE

Effective job analyses benefit the school employees in several ways. A clear assignment serves to help the employee initiate his or her own initiative toward the accomplishment of job purposes. As a result, the employee has a greater feeling of *ownership* of the position and more responsibility for producing quality results. The workers' health and safety considerations are given greater protection when the effects of the work on the worker are known. Work hours, safety measures, sanitation policies, protection standards, and healthy working environments are identified, implemented, and controlled.

The completion of a job analysis is an important planning task and the first step in developing a job description for the specific position at hand. The employee first completes the job analysis, and then it is followed by a verification by the appropriate supervisor.

The supervisor examines the completed job analysis and then responds to questions such as the following: (1) Is the position in question essentially accurate? (2) What important activities of the job were omitted or should not have been included in the analysis? (3) Are the skill requirements listed by the worker adequate for the position? If not what additional knowledge/skills should be added? (4) Is the present classification for the position correct? Why or why not? (5) In view of the qualification and conditions related to the position, what specific orientation/preparation might be important for any new worker in the position? (5) What other observations and/or recommendations might you have or find necessary for the position at hand?

A meeting is held by the worker and supervisor to discuss the job analysis and the supervisor's follow-up report. Mutual agreements are underscored and differences are reconciled as fits the case. As a result, cooperative relationships are fostered and the worker's confidence in his or her work is enhanced.

PRIMARY CONTENTS OF A JOB ANALYSIS

The sections/contents of a job analysis commonly include information within seven specific sections that focus on the following:

(1) The job itself—its purpose, description, tasks, standards, work/time factors, materials/tools required, expected outcomes, and so forth

(2) Employee job qualifications—degrees/certifications required; special knowledge; skills and competencies needed; experience required; supervisory expectations; mental, emotional, and physical requirements; judgment capabilities; and leadership responsibilities

(3) The effects of the work requirements on the job holder—personal relationships, stress components, internal/external clientele demands, job retention, health/safety factors, positive/negative features

(4) Work schedule—nature of the job activities and time allotments relative to the job; work schedule, including day/night assignments; indoor/outdoor settings; flexibility of work/time arrangements; home work arrangements, production time scheduling

(5) The work environment/climate—job climate factors, hazards, working environment, job/position workload factors, job characteristics and conditions (sitting, standing, moving, lifting, monotony), production expectations

(6) Job/personnel relationships—supervision given, supervision received, support services, performance evaluations, reporting requirements, communication channels/processes, line relationships, unit relationships

(7) Employment compensation and benefits—the terms of employment, including salary, fringe benefits, contract time specifications, merit programs, promotion procedures, improvement requirements and opportunities, and continuous employment clarification

JOB ANALYSIS AND LEVELS OF RESPONSIBILITY, KNOWLEDGE/SKILLS, AND SUPERVISION

Although a job analysis commonly would include the process of planning, required knowledge, supervision, and required affective characteristics such as judgment and personnel relationships, the level of these factors must be determined. In the following section, only a few planning levels are shown; planning levels might include as many as six steps or more as fits the case. Note that level 3 skips two planning levels and includes the sixth, top, level in the analysis.

Level 1, the lowest level, might be found in a position where only simple routine procedures have to be followed; no specific planning is required.

Level 2, requires simple routine planning activities consisting of little or no complexity.

Level 3, requires the coordination/utilization of some work activities that commonly are straightforward and short range in nature. Supervisory instructions and guidelines are available for the worker to utilize.

Level 6, the highest level, requires primary planning knowledge and skills that involve complex and varied work situations. Planning for the most part is long range and requires giving attention to the future mission of the organiza-tion. Although the organization commonly has a mission statement, level 6 planning involves the organization's vision statement.

Similarly, other job factors such as knowledge/skill, decision making, judgment, and supervision should be developed in relation to job levels. For example, level 1 for knowledge/skill might read, "Has common knowledge/skills of the position that has relatively simple operations." Level 6, the high-est level, might read, "Possesses a high quality of knowledge and skills for the major process of the position and the position's relationship to other posi-tions in the network". Is able to identify and set forth procedures for meeting the required standards for the position's effectiveness.

Why Job Analysis Is Necessary and Important: Who Benefits?

Not only the position holder but most everyone benefits by the completion of a job analysis. Are the position holder and his or her supervisor on the same page regarding the purposes, facilitators, and inhibitors of the job; the actual knowledge and skills required; the effects of the work on the position holder; and how the position relates to other positions in the system and to the primary goals of the unit and/or school system? If not, the employee's effec-tiveness is problematic. Specifically, the school district and its administrative officials benefit by a position analysis by

- learning about the actual job responsibilities that the work is or is not accomplishing;
- understanding what the position holder believes to be the primary purposes of his or her work results and how these perceptions compare to those of the position's supervisor;
- gaining an understanding of the knowledge and skills required in the job and results in the organization's ability to develop a meaningful position description;
- gaining insight into the needed improvements in job performance;
- understanding the climate within the job and its effects on the worker's accomplishments;
- understanding the nature of the job and its relationships to other jobs within the school system;
- identifying time factors related to task completion;
- identifying the actual tasks that are encompassed in the specific job;
- assessing the behavior patterns of the employee relative to the performance of the job;
- identifying the affective characteristics and the cognitive characteristics of a high-quality employee in the job.

The position holder benefits as well by participating in a job analysis in that the activity provides

- guidance for focusing on the primary purposes of the position and the relevance of the position activities;
- insight into the effects of the work and into the work climate;
- an opportunity for the employee to participate in the ongoing development/ changes in the position's activities and the outcomes of major importance;
- insight into the actions needed to foster a relevant work environment and one that contributes most beneficially to the organization's goals and objectives;
- a mutual understanding between the employee and supervisor(s) as to the nature of the job and its importance to the organization;
- an enriched opportunity for the employee to move ahead and use his or her knowledge and talents in the accomplishment of the position's purposes;
- definite, systematic, and relevant information/data for determining the actual worth of the position;
- relevant information to utilize in the recruiting, selection, placement, development, and compensation of personnel;
- clarification concerning the responsibility, accountability, and related authority of the position and its relationships to other positions/personnel in the position's network and the overall school system.

COMPETENCY-BASED REQUIREMENTS OF THE HR DIRECTOR'S POSITION

Both job analysis and competency-based performance concepts contribute essentially to the HR director's position design and analysis. *Competency-based performance* serves to identify the primary tasks, competencies, and indicators of competencies as related to the work of the HR director. A *task* is viewed as a primary responsibility, requirement, or assignment of the human resources director's role. The specific knowledge/skills and abilities required for accomplishing the task are termed *competencies.* The expected outcomes, products, and overt behaviors demonstrated by the director are the *indicators of competencies.* That is, indicators reveal the extent to which the tasks are being performed.

A selected listing of the tasks, competencies, and indicators of competency of the HR director is presented in Table 1.2. Competency-based performance listings serve several beneficial purposes, including the evaluation and assessment of performance expectations and effectiveness. Such listings should be viewed as adaptive (rather than adoptive) to the varying administrative situations that exist in school districts.

Table 1.2. Selected Tasks/Competencies for the Human Resources Director's Position

Human Resources Director

TASK—RECRUITMENT/SELECTION

1.0 To recruit/select qualified applicants (p)

    1.1 Ability to identify primary sources of applicants/candidates
    1.2 Ability to plan and organize recruitment and selection processes

2.0 To screen/interview applicants for positions (p)

    2.1 Ability to relate specific functions to needs/purposes of the school/district
    2.2 Ability to interview and identify candidates that possess high-quality qualifications for the position in question

3.0 To select the best qualified candidate(s) for the given position (s)

    3.1 Ability to identify the qualities of a given position
    3.2 Ability to demonstrate the school and school district's best qualities and opportunities for professional and classified personnel

4.0 To complete job analyses and provide follow-up job descriptions(s)

    4.1 Ability to implement the job analysis procedure and cooperate in the completion of job descriptions
    4.2 Ability to keep abreast of job changes and understand how to improve related practices

TASK—STAFF ORIENTATION AND DEVELOPMENT

5.0 To plan, organize, and implement an ongoing orientation and professional program for personnel new to the school(s)

    5.1 Ability to determine the needs and problems encountered by personnel new to the school
    5.2 Ability to plan, organize, implement, and assess an ongoing program of activities for the purpose of personnel and program change and development
    5.3 Ability to understand the nature of the school district's vision statement and address these purposes in the provision of personnel development programs
    5.4 Ability to understand and practice the importance of providing a variety of professional development activities for retaining the personnel in the school
    5.5 Ability to promote and implement human resources values by planning and administering HR programs and directing staff issues/needs

TASK—WAGE AND SALARY ADMINISTRATION

6.0 To assist in the development of the district-appropriate policy on wages and salaries(s)

6.1 Ability to know the significance of economic, social-cultural factors in appropriate/effective wage and salary programs

6.2 Ability to implement and administer the fringe benefits program for professional and classified personnel

6.3 Ability to understand and implement the financial requirements of state and federal agencies, including state and school board policies on professional negotiations

TASK—CONTRACTUAL RELATIONSHIPS AND CONDITIONS OF EMPLOYMENT

7.0 To aid contractual agreements and employee conditions of employment(s)

7.1 Ability to know and understand federal, state, court, and school board laws, statutes, rulings, and policies related to personnel administration

7.2 Ability to establish administrative procedures for processing such personnel matters as leaves, transfers, evaluations, continuation of employment, retirement, and related personnel considerations

7.3 Ability to design and implement a process for obtaining a pool of qualified substitutes for employee absences

7.4 Ability to travel within the complex of the school community and externally for purposes of communication, research, and personnel development

TASK—DEVELOPMENT OF PERSONNEL POLICIES

8.0 To develop and revise drafts of personnel policies for consideration of district officers and adoption by the school board(s)

8.1 Ability to plan and organize for policy development

8.2 Ability to assimilate legal actions by the state and school board and draft related policies

8.3 Ability to know and understand the difference between school board policy and administrative regulations

TASK—PROMOTION OF SCHOOL CLIMATE

9.0 To establish and develop a positive climate within the school district(s)

9.1 Ability to provide leadership in developing a healthy climate within the school district that results in high morale and positive student achievement

9.2 Ability to foster a climate of self-renewal by personally establishing improvement projects and programs cooperatively with school personnel and the school community

Skill level legend: 1, familiarity (awareness); 2, understanding (knowledge of its relevance); 3, application (can apply it in practice); p, primary; s, shared.

Competency-based statements commonly includes other major tasks, such as negotiations and maintenance of agreement provisions, administration of the human resources unit, administration responsibilities (communications and relationships), personnel legal responsibilities, classified personnel, and management change.

THE HUMAN RESOURCES DIRECTOR'S JOB DESCRIPTION

The processes of personnel evaluation, funding, hiring, and others differ based on the size of school districts, personnel needs, business/financial arrangements, and other factors. In some school districts, the HR director is responsible for either the professional staff or the classified staff. In others, he or she assumes the responsibility for both employee groups. The following example of such a description illustrates the comprehensiveness of the role and shows the major components of a position description that would be appropriate as a guide for any school district. The key is the *adaptation* rather than the *adoption* of the position description set forth below.

EXAMPLE DESCRIPTION OF A DIRECTOR OF HUMAN RESOURCES POSITION

LAFAYETTE SCHOOL DISTRICT POSITION DESCRIPTION

POSITION TITLE: Director of Human Resources
GUIDING STATEMENT OF POSITION PURPOSE

To plan, coordinate, and supervise the operation of the human resources function of the school district in such a way as to enhance the morale of the school district's personnel, promote the overall quality of the school system, and maximize the educational opportunities for students and quality of teaching throughout the school system.

Position Qualifications (r, required; p, preferred; s, shared)

1. Experience as a school teacher (p)
2. Experience in educational administration or related personnel work in business/industrial management (r)
3. Master's degree in educational administration or related field (r) or doctoral degree (p)
4. Record of positive working relationships in previous employment (r)
5. Knowledge of the major processes of the human resources function in organizations, including recruitment, selection, orientation, placement,

development, evaluation, stability, security, compensation, and other
related processes (r)
6. Working knowledge of personnel salary and benefits in organizations (r)
7. Knowledge of the legal requirements within the human resources function (r)
8. Experience in contract relations, including professional negotiations (s)
9. Ability to foster a positive climate within the school system (s)
10. Drafting and recommending new and revised personnel policies (s)
11. Ability to make decisions in a variety of situations encountered in the HR
function (p)

Immediate Supervisor

School district assistant superintendent or superintendent of schools

Supervision Given

Employees assigned to the human resources department (note: in some school
districts, the HR director is also the assistant superintendent of schools; in such
cases, supervision responsibilities are extended within the school district).

Major Position Responsibilities

1. Supervises and Directs:
   a. Supervises the planning and analysis of personnel needs of the school
      district
   b. Plans and implements the recruitment program for certificated and
      classified personnel
   c. Screens and processes (with others) all employee candidates for sub-
      mission to the school superintendent and ultimately to the school board
   d. Leads in the phases of the human resources function that center on
      records and reports budget considerations, employment placements
      (classified and professional), contract administration, payroll admin-
      istration (with business office), benefits program, certification and
      licensing, negotiations, and related processes
   e. Supervises selection and assignment of substitute teachers
   f. Supervises salary and contract administration

2. Evaluation Responsibilities:
   a. Evaluates prospective teacher and administrative applicants in coopera-
      tion with appropriate others
   b. Evaluates all classified personnel in cooperation with other department
      heads
   c. Evaluates substitute teacher applicants and their performance in coop-
      eration with appropriate others, such as the school principal

d. Reviews ongoing personnel procedures and practices
e. Reviews personnel policies in practice
f. Evaluates school administrative personnel with appropriate others

3. Coordinates and/or Assists:
   a. In the selection of certificated and classified personnel
   b. In the review of requests for transfer, leaves, or promotion of personnel
   c. In the negotiations (meet and confer) process
   d. As an administrative representative to the negotiations process
   e. As a counselor and advisor in personnel matters relating to insubordination, dismissal, and other legal/sensitive matters
   f. In the evaluation and assessment of issues, problems, and changes within the human resources function
   g. In research studies related to human resources processes, including salary and benefits, change management, and legal matters
   h. In the salary and benefits process for certificated and classified personnel
   i. In the establishment of personnel policy and administrative regulations
   j. As a member of the superintendent's cabinet
   k. In the management of strategic staffing plans
   l. In providing consultation and administration of the school district's employee relations program
   m. In preparing and reporting on HR metrics for the purpose of assessing needs and achievements
   n. In using technology to promote efficiency and enhance the results of all human resources activities
   o. In the matters of employee discipline, including the legal considerations of these matters

4. Develops and Maintains:
   a. Positive affective skills for fostering effective interpersonal skills
   b. Up-to-date information concerning management changes and current research in the function of human resources
   c. High-level communication skills with administrators, staff members, students, and the school community
   d. Appropriate and timely personnel reports
   e. An ongoing procedure for keeping the school officials and members of the school board fully informed of issues, needs, accomplishments, and plans in relation to the personnel function
   f. An updated personnel handbook for school personnel, including a security guide for appropriate actions in case of emergencies and other troublesome activities
   g. A meaningful program for the retention of talent within the school district

5. Related Assignments/Responsibilities:
   a. Engages in activities that serve to promote and secure the rights of all employees within the school system
   b. Serves as a hearing officer on employee appeals of disciplinary matters and coordinates district grievance and complaint hearings
   c. Reviews all staff evaluations and makes recommendations for suspending, terminating, or continuing the employment of school district personnel
   d. Maintains a planned program for professional growth and development of personnel

WHY IS CHANGE MANAGEMENT AT THE TOP OF THE LIST OF HR CHALLENGES?

We asked a small group of human resources directors "what was happening today in their field of work." The immediate answer was "change." University Alliance (2016, March 21) reported a study conducted by PricewaterhouseCoopers on behalf of the World Federation of Personnel Management Associations. Ten leading human resources management challenges were identified. Forty-eight percent of the participating companies named change management as the number one challenge facing them. This finding underscores the importance of the need for an intensified focus on training to develop the required competencies to deal with change management.

"Change management (CM) refers to any approach to transitioning individuals, teams, and organizations using methods intended to re-direct the use of resources, business process, budget allocations, or other modes of operations that significantly reshape a company or organization" (Wikipedia, 2016, p. 1). Effective *change management* is a planned and designed method used to be certain that changes are thoughtfully implemented in order to result in desired benefits. Internal change comes about when evaluation and assessment of the school district's education metrics reveal program gaps and/or unproductive procedures being practiced.

As Fowler (2016) states: "Overloading a single metric with multiple purposes causes many problems, particularly when dealing with knowledge work such as software. Metrics are simplifications of much more complex attributes. The cost of simplifying complexity comes at the cost of losing sight of the real end goal, and ends in suboptimal results" (p. 2). Fowler contends that the problem rests in the use of single-loop learning rather than using double-loop leaning. Double-loop learning includes the process of questioning whether operating norms are appropriate. Double-loop learning gives the important opportunity to question the intended goal.

THE SIGNIFICANCE OF DOUBLE-LOOP LEARNING

Morgan illustrates double-loop learning as shown in Figure 1.1. *Single-loop learning* is illustrated in steps 1, 2, and 3. In step 1, the process of sensing, scanning, and monitoring the environment is completed. In step 2, the information gathered in step 1 is compared with operating norms. The final step, step 3, is the process of initiating appropriate action. In double-loop learning, step 2a is added whereby the vital process of questioning whether operating norms are appropriate is addressed. This additional step serves the possibility that self-adjustment could take place by determining the appropriate norms for the situation at hand. That is, the organization is able to learn in an ongoing way. Self-organization is possible. The organization can detect and correct errors in operating norms, and it is able to affect the metrics (standards) that guide comprehensive operations (Morgan, 1987).

We caution against using metrics and setting goals for long periods of review of achievement gaps. Assume that 50% of fifth-grade students were reading below grade level and you set the target for 100% of all fifth-grade students to be reading at grade level within one year. After one year, 52% of the fifth-grade students were reading below grade level. You had one whole year to meet your target and did not achieve it. Fowler (2016) notes that the risk and cost of failure is likely to increase the longer the target period lasts. As he points out, failing to make enough progress in a week is much less significant than failing to make enough progress over a year.

The recommendation is to have much shorter review periods that provide many more opportunities to re-plan and change; shorter review periods create more chances to react with known data and change accordingly. This recommendation is our point. Double-loop learning and wise use of metrics, as shown in Figure 1.1, help school personnel to keep focus on the real goal(s) and the direction for collecting meaningful data that lead to positive change and achievement of real purposes.

External change is brought about by such events as federal/state mandates, decisions of court cases, societal/cultural factors, economic influences, and other unforeseen external circumstances. Skelsey (2013) points out that rapid growth and development of technology have motivated external change innovations rather than internal factors. If the organization does not adapt, it is likely that it will find itself unable to compete and thus is left behind. Myrtle (2016) speaks of emerging trends in human resources management that include political, economic, social, and technological trends. Increased demands for transparency in government and organizations are an example of an emerging political trend.

As noted by Norton (2015), contemporary issues and problems faced by educational leaders must be viewed as *symptoms of change*. The symptoms

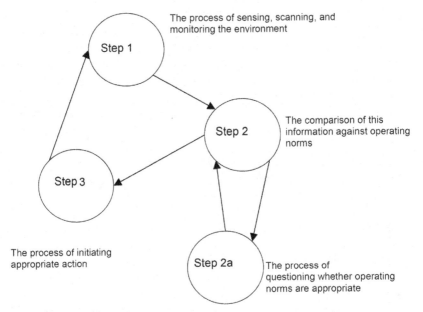

Figure 1.1.   Single- and Double-Loop Learning

Source: Gareth Morgan, *Images of Organization* (1987). Newbury Park, CA: Sage Publications. Reprinted by permission.

are administrative tasks that must be attacked by implementing the knowledge and skills for which the administrator was hired, taking the leadership of resolving the issues/problems of ongoing change. The human resources function in education historically has faced the problem of personnel turnover. Its ongoing occurrence has led to the matter of turnover being considered as "just the way it is" and "that's nothing new." Yet, the instability in the educational workforce militates against the purpose of achieving high levels of educational services.

Later chapters focus on the problem of staff changes and instability in the workforce. *Onboarding* is discussed later in further detail. Onboarding is the process of organizational socialization and a way new employees acquire the necessary knowledge, skills, and behaviors to become effective in the school and school system. The outcomes of effective onboarding are seen in positive job satisfaction, improved work performance, greater commitment, reduction in job stress, and high levels of personnel retention (Definitions, 2016).

Key Chapter Ideas and Recommendations

• Historically, the human resources function has focused on the concept of human relationships and the fact that schools are people. People are viewed as organizational assets as opposed to expenditures.

- HR trends center attention on change management as related to remaining vital and competitive in a diversified world. Retention of talent, diversity in the workplace, funding, appropriate use of metrics, evolving technology, work-life balance, career development, and concerns relative to competitive educational programs are among the major concerns of contemporary human resources directors in education.
- The position of human resources director must deal with a wide variety of processes. Nevertheless, the recruitment, selection, and retention of qualified personnel remain a high priority.
- Preparation programs for aspiring human resources leaders must be recalibrated and improved. A limited percentage of practicing human resources directors report that they believe that they were well prepared to assume the position of director.
- The need to come to grips with the appropriate title for the person directing the human resources function for the school district is imperative. For purposes of understanding and relational communication, one title would prove beneficial. Director of human resources is the most common title for the position nationally. Most everyone understands the titles of teacher, school principal, superintendent of schools, and instructional supervisor. Yet, in one state study of human resources directors, twenty-three different titles of the position were listed.
- The turnover in the HR directorship militates against effectiveness and stability in the position. In one state study, only 25% of the district HR administrators had served for at least four to five years in the role.
- The process of position analysis is recommended for its many benefits for both the school district's employees and its administrative personnel. Both basic and empirical research has found that the process of job analysis is one of the most promising ways to foster personnel improvement and effective supervisory relationships.

DISCUSSION QUESTIONS

1. This chapter emphasizes the vital importance of human relationships in the human resources function in education. Consider the design and analysis aspects of the HR director's role as described throughout the chapter. Then describe just how the human relations concept is actually revealed in current practice.

2. Studies related to preparation for the position of human resources director in education reveal that a relatively low percentage of directors believe that they were well prepared to assume the responsibilities of the role. Take time to set forth what needs to be done to obviate this problem. For example, what changes might you recommend in the preparation programs in higher education?

3. Instability in the human resources function is affected by the fact that turnover in the HR director's role is problematic. What, in your opinion, are the underlying reasons for high turnover in this important administrative role in school districts?

4. Assume that you are serving as the HR director in your school district. A school principal in the school district informs you that he is a finalist for a HR director's position in another school district. He asks for your thoughts about the requirements of the role and what essential knowledge and skills are of special importance. What response would you give to this individual?

5. Review the chapter's discussion of double-loop learning. What is this concept all about? How does double-loop learning fit into the design and analysis of the work of the human resources director?

6. List several changes that are taking place in your school community that are having an impact on the administration of the human resources function in your school district. What is the nature of these changes and what is being done to meet these changes?

7. Turn back to Figure 1.1. Explain step 2a in the diagram. What happens when step 2a is implemented? What questions are asked? What data are assessed?

CASE STUDIES

Case 1.1   Let's Just Forget about Wasting Time on Job Descriptions

Superintendent Thomas Scott asked Romero Ortiz, director of human resources, to meet him in the office to discuss a matter.

When Ortiz arrived for the meeting, the superintendent commented: "Romero, we have a problem on our hands. The school board has asked that we complete job descriptions for each job we have for classified personnel. Since we have job grade levels for every job family, this will be a task and a half."

"Does the board realize just how many job classifications we have in the district?" asked Ortiz. "Didn't the board ask us to do something like this several months ago?"

"Yeah," responded Superintendent Scott, "but I convinced them that job descriptions were just ways to freeze a job in place. Employees generally do just what the description sets forth and nothing more. It stifles employee creativity. Nevertheless, I am expected to report back on this matter at the next board meeting."

"Well, let me give some thought to this matter and I will get back to you soon. At least I might be able to recommend a plan of action," said Romero.

DISCUSSION EXERCISE

1. In a class situation, students should divide into groups of four to six people. If considered by individuals, students should assume the role of human resources director, Romero Ortiz, and set forth a follow-up plan for consideration by Superintendent Scott. Keep the complexity of the school board's request and how the task could be accomplished over a reasonable time to benefit the school board, administration, and the district's employees.
2. Give some thought to the comment by Superintendent Scott that relative job descriptions merely serve to freeze a job in place. How might the HR director avoid such a result?

REFERENCES

Definitions (2016, April 9). *What does onboarding mean?* From the Web: http://www.definitions.net/definition /onboarding

Deloitte Development LLC (2016). *Global human capital trends 2016: The new organization: Different by design.* Phoenix, AZ: author.

Follett, M. P. (1924). *Creative experience.* New York: Longmans, Green.

Fowler, M. (2016, March 31). *An appropriate use of metrics.* From the Web: http://martinfowler.com/articles/useOfMetrics.html

Herzberg, F., Mausner, B., & Snyderman, B. (1959). *The motivation to work.* New York: Wiley.

Likert, Rensis (1967). *The human organization.* New York: McGraw-Hill.

McGregor, D. (1960). *The human side of enterprise.* New York: McGraw-Hill.

Morgan, G. (1987a). *Images of organization.* Newbury Park, CA: Sage.

Morgan, G. (1987b). *Images of organization.* Newbury Park, CA: Sage.

Myrtle, R. C. (2016). *Emerging trends in human resources management (2016).* USC Price. Sol Price School of Public Policy. USC University of Public Policy. University of Southern California.

Norton, M. S. (2008). *Human resources administration for educational leaders.* Thousand Oaks, CA: Sage.

Norton, M. S. (2015). *The changing landscape of school leadership: Recalibrating the school principalship.* Lanham, MD: Rowman & Littlefield.

Public Administration (2016, March 26). *Public administration.* From the Web: en.wikipedia.org/wiki/publicadministration

Skelsey, D. (2013). *Why do people resist change in business?* ProjectLaneways.com.au/our—promise

Tead, O., & Metcalf, H. C. (1920). *Personnel administration.* New York: McGraw-Hill.

University Alliance (2016). *Human resources challenges.* Powered by Bisk on behalf of Villanova University. From the web: villanovau.com/resources/hr/management-

Wikipedia (2016). Definition of change management. In *Change Management.* From the web: en.wikipedia.org/wiki/change—management_challenges/#.WHiClWcGiw

Young, I. P. (2008). *The human resources function in educational administration* (9th ed.). Upper Saddle River, N. J.: Pearson Merrill Prentice-Hall.

Chapter 2

The Essentials of Human Resources
Workplace Planning and Organization

Primary chapter goal: To underscore the vital importance of planning and organizational development for effective human resources allocation and for integrating human resources planning into the school district's strategic plan.

UNDERSTANDING PLANNING AS A STRATEGIC TOOL FOR SOUND PROGRAM ADMINISTRATION AND DEVELOPMENT

A chapter on planning and organization? Isn't that old hat? We submit that it is high on the list of the most important things that human resources directors must do to meet the challenges of ongoing change. The process of planning serves as the foundation for all of the other processes of the human resources function. Without effective planning, the human resources function will not be effective. But planning is much more than just deciding what to do.

Planning is a strategic process that ties closely to change management. It is the foundational process by which the school board and administration can evaluate and assess the effectiveness of personnel who must perform the required tasks that are needed to achieve the school district's goals and objectives. In the following section, we discuss the six primary activities of planning: *forecasting, designing, strategizing, organizing, participating*, and *cooperative collaborating*. Planning can be either short range or long range.

Effective planning encourages responsive administration, fosters employee commitment, and enables administrators to set goals and determine standards that are directed toward maximizing human performance. We submit that the time and effort utilized in the planning process will pay beneficial dividends in results related to recruitment, selection, orientation, development, and other primary human resources processes.

Short-range planning tends to be reactive in that it is commonly a response to an immediate issue/need. Long-range planning is more proactive in that it considers issues/needs in a more comprehensive manner that answers the question, "What must we do now to reach the goals and objectives that we envision for our future?" Planning and implementation go hand in hand. A plan in itself is static; a plan to be beneficial must be implemented. Implementing a program without a plan is little more than a shot in the dark; the program becomes a directionless activity. There is little chance that the program will result in beneficial results.

THE ACTIVITY OF FORECASTING: THE HR DIRECTOR'S CRYSTAL BALL

Forecasting involves looking toward the future and determining, evaluating, and assessing probabilities. Human resources forecasts serve the vital foundation for the determination of personnel needs due to growth in student enrollment and the probabilities of staff mixes. Not only must future personnel numbers be projected relative to growth in student enrollment, but the considerations of attrition loom important due to employees leaving the school system, moving to other positions in the school system, or being released due to decreases in student enrollment.

Guesswork relative to such projections leads to one unfortunate result: trouble. A thoughtful forecast of personnel changes provides the human resources administration with beneficial information that can be used to guide employment decisions and serves to enhance the overall strategic objectives of the HR function and the school system.

Personnel turnover in school systems commonly is viewed as one of its most serious problems. The reasons for turnover are many but are simply attributed to the shifting that takes place in the school system's workforce. That is, every individual who leaves the school system, regardless of the reason, is a number in the turnover statistic (TS). In this sense, if a school employed 600 certificated personnel and 120 of them left at the end of the year, the turnover rate is calculated by dividing the number of certified employees that left the school system at the end of the year (TS) by the total number of certificated employees (120): (TS divided by TCE = percentage of turnover), or 600 divided by 120 = 0.20 or 20%.

Research on turnover in school systems nationally commonly reports the figure at 20% to 33% after one year and approximately 40% to 50% after five years. Consider a situation whereby a group of 125 new teachers were hired.

After the very first year of their service, twenty-five to forty-two of that group will leave the system. Within five years, approximately fifty to sixty-three employees of that same group will leave the system. Replacement problems, including financial costs, are problematic. It isn't just a matter of calling in a new teacher. Costs of advertising for the replacement position, travel, clerical services, printing of recruitment materials, and personnel services and other related expenses are necessary.

As one director of classified personnel explained, just as we spend time and money for the training of a new employee, all too often the employee leaves for a better paying job and our training expenses have gone for naught. The director went on to say that "sometimes I think that worker retention is more important than worker recruitment." Replacing a certificated teacher has been calculated to cost 25% of each person's salary (Norton, 2008). Replacing each of twenty-five new teachers leaving at the end of their first year with an average salary of $36,000 per year would be an approximate turnover cost of $225,000, money that could be well spent in other programs of the school system.

FORECASTING FOR MEETING HUMAN RESOURCES PURPOSES

Forecasting serves to provide data for determining personnel needs, providing a basis for assessing productivity levels, helping to avoid the financial problems related to over-hiring, monitoring the attrition of personnel in relation to resignations, retirements, and movements to other district positions and personnel leaves, and avoid the troublesome outcomes of guesswork. The HR director uses judgmental strategies to determine such personnel information as hiring data, dismissal statistics, and turnover results. *Vacancy analysis* is one example of judgmental techniques; it focuses on determining employee movements over both short-range and long-range time periods.

Quantitative techniques of forecasting center on determining the school district's employee supply. It is beyond the scope of this chapter to discuss the many options available for this purpose. Nevertheless, we will present a common method of forecasting employee needs in the next section of the chapter.

THE ACTIVITY OF DESIGNING

The activity of designing is the human resource director's strategy of establishing priorities for implementation. The HR director necessarily must give

serious thought to purposes. What is the guiding purpose(s) of the HR function? Why does the school district's human resources unit exist? Are its purposes just to recruit, select, orient, and develop personnel? We submit that the
primary purpose of the HR function is the same as that of the school district:
schools exist of and for their students. That is, the HR function exists for *student reasons*. Therefore, we design creative plans of action for accomplishing
goals and objectives that center on *student reasons*.

The HR processes of recruiting, selecting, orienting, and developing and
all other HR processes are based on the purpose of providing the optimal
learning program for students in the school district. Our planning designs
focus on actions plans that result in the very best possible applicants for
positions within the school district. We set forth action plans not only to hire
personnel but to retain the employee talent in the school district. We support
a variety of growth and development activities for personnel not only for
continuous improvement but to meet the growth expectations that quality
performers personally want and demand.

Markovian analysis is a popular quantitative strategy for forecasting
employee supply. Assume that your school system employed 1,335 certificated personnel, including 275 primary teachers, 225 intermediate-level
teachers, 200 upper-level teachers, 475 secondary teachers, 65 supervisory
personnel, and 95 administrators. Table 2.1 shows these figures in columns
a and *b*. Columns *c* through *h* show the probability factors for each of the
classifications. The probability factors were determined by calculating the
average movement data during a period of time such as the last five years.
Average data would be quite stable over the years unless some major change
in school district growth or population decline took place.

Column *c* shows a probability of 0.75 (75%) of the primary teachers
remaining on the job for the forthcoming year. Ten percent of the primary

Table 2.1. Markovian Analysis of Human Resources Attrition

Role	Current	Primary	Intermediate	Upper	Secondary	Super.	Admin.	Projection
a	b	c	d	e	f	g	h	i
Primary	275	0.75	0.10	0.05			0.01	240
Intermediate	225	0.10	0.75	0.10				202
Upper	200	0.06	0.09	0.75		0.02		188
Secondary	475			0.06	0.75			368
Supervisors	65	0.02			0.02	0.88		70
Administrators	95			0.01	0.05	0.05	0.83	94
Exit		0.07	0.06	0.03	0.21	0.05	0.06	148

teachers move to the intermediate grades; 5% (0.05) move to the upper grades, 1% (0.01) move to an administrative position, and 9% (0.09) leave the school system. In a similar manner, 2% (0.02) of the secondary teachers move to the upper grades, 78% (0.78) remain for the next year, 1% (0.01) move to a supervisory position, 1% (0.01) move to an administrative role, and 18% (0.18) exit the school system. Column *i* projects the following year's numbers by grade levels and positions.

FORECASTING STUDENT ENROLLMENTS

Technology has made possible numerous strategies for forecasting student enrollment. For example, Rowman & Littlefield published a book some time ago (Smith, 2005) that runs on any Windows-platform computer with Microsoft Excel version 5.0 or later. It also runs on a Macintosh with Excel 98. According to Smith, EnrollForecast for Excel generates a five-year forecast for K-12 student enrollment.

Forecasting techniques used by school districts include quantitative techniques and qualitative techniques. Qualitative forecasting uses the school district's historical enrollment data that focus on curve fitting. Casual models also rely on historical enrollment data and other subjective parameters, including qualitative judgments. Qualitative techniques commonly use survey data to determine the status of student numbers. A common forecast method for school districts historically has been the *cohort survival* method. This method is based on the assumption that related statistics such as school district growth will remain similar to what they have been over the years.

Consider the following example. Over a period of ten years, an average of 95% of the kindergarten students of the Wymore School District move on to grade one. Similarly, 93% of the district's first graders moved on to grade during the same ten-year time period. If the Wymore School District presently had 600 students in kindergarten, the forecast for next year's grade one enrollment would be 570 students. The second-grade forecast for the following year would be 530 students. It is obvious that the accuracy of forecasting is highest when determined one year in advance as opposed to five or ten years ahead in time.

Kindergarten enrollment projections also can be forecast using average cohort retention ratios. Table 2.2 illustrates projections for a five-year time period from 2017 to 2022. The cohort retention ratio is calculated by dividing the kindergarten enrollment by the number of births for any specific year.

Table 2.2.   Enrollment Numbers Projected for Kindergarten

Year of Birth	Number of Births	Kindergarten Year	Kindergarten Enrollment	Cohort Retention Ratio
2012	3,400	2017	3,380	0.9941
2013	3,450	2018	3,401	0.9858
2014	3,600	2003	3,503	0.9731
2015	3,701	2004	3,650	0.9862
2016	3,800	2005	3,701	0.9739
2017	4,000	2006		

When the kindergarten enrollment is divided by the number of births for any specific year, the result is the cohort retention ratio (e.g., 2012: 3,380 divided by 3,400 = 0.9941). What about forecasting the student enrollment for 2022? The forecasted 2022 kindergarten enrollment is calculated as follows. Find the average cohort retention ratio by adding the five previous ratios and then divide the result by 5. The average cohort ration is 0.9826. Next, multiply the number of births five years previously, 4,000, by the mean enrollment ratio, 0.9826. The 2022 kindergarten enrollment forecast is 3,930.

THE DESIGNING ACTIVITY

The *designing activity* is the implementation of actions plans that are directed by the stated goals and objectives of the human resources function. The director of the human resources function must ask himself or herself the following questions: "Why does the human resources function exist?" and "What is the main reason for our being here?" As previously noted, we take the position that the human resources function exists for the same primary reason that the school districts exists: because of and for the students enrolled in the school district.

We urge human resources directors and their staff to give serious thought to the foregoing student reasons for their existence. What do we as human resources leaders stand for? What characteristics and/or descriptors best describe our function? We submit that the quality of the school district's administrators, professional personnel, and classified staff personnel is directly related to the quality of our school district's programs and student achievement. The goals and objectives of the HR function must tie inextricably to the goals of the school district's student purposes.

A PLAN FOR RETAINING EMPLOYEE TALENT

Consider the designing of an action program for retaining employee talent within the school district. What administrative knowledge and skills are needed relative to designing a talent retention plan? School districts are inextricably influenced by the present open talent economy. *Talent management* centers on efforts to retain quality personnel and to develop succession planning. For example, your design should include the establishment of employee performance objectives. Such planning includes the cooperative discussion between the employee(s) and supervisor relative to the primary purposes of the work itself. An effective design establishes accountability; the emphasis is placed in the expected end results of the work.

An employee individual development plan is an important aspect of the design. How are the end results evaluated and assessed? What administrative support will be provided? Is attention given to the "rewards" for individual performance outcomes? What must be done to keep the school district's talent from jumping ship? Empirical evidence suggests that 9 to 5 jobs are disappearing. What flexible work options might be successful in K-12 school districts? What leadership is needed relative to the implementation of equitable workload assignments for teachers and support personnel? Who is giving major attention to teacher workload in schools?

CHAPTER SNAPSHOT—DO TEACHERS ACTUALLY DO THIS EVERY DAY?

Southeast High School scheduled a scientist for teacher day once each semester. Community members employed in science-related positions in the community would replace the school's science teachers for one entire day. The scientists would give students relevant information about their career work, and teachers would participate in improvement program activities in a school setting or participate in conferences, workshops, or other activities relative to their teaching responsibilities. The school day was from 8:30 to 3:30 with one-half hour for lunch.

Paul Henson was the chief engineer for the local telephone company. He met with one class of general science, two classes of general biology, one class of physics, and one class of chemistry. Of course, Paul did not teach the actual subject matter of the respective classes; rather, he emphasized the importance of science in the various facets of the telephone company's work.

At the end of the scientist-for-teacher-day activity, Paul was accompanied to the teachers' lounge for refreshments. He entered the lounge, sat back in his chair, and said, "Do teachers actually do this every day?"

Strategizing centers on the activities required to reach desired goals and objectives. Morgan (1986) suggests that the strategy activity answers the question, "What kind of strategy is being employed by the organization?" (p. 62). Is the organization merely reacting to whatever change comes along or does its strategy activity adopt an innovative, future-looking position whereby searches for new opportunities loom important for meeting the tasks that accompany on-going change? "Strategic HR planning is a dynamic process for helping a school system shape its future. . . Strategic planning serves to tie the specific objectives of the HR function to the overall purposes and objectives of the school system" (Norton, 1968, p. 80).

Strategizing serves the school system in general and the HR function specifically in shaping its own future as opposed to merely reacting to organizational change as it occurs. Effective strategizing include the following features: comprehensive (all school units involved); continuous (part of the school system's planning cycle); multi-year planning arrangement (one to five years); and flexible (modification as required by internal and external environment changes).

ORGANIZING AND STRATEGIC DECISION MAKING

Organizing is the activity of using a systematic approach to the changes that are inevitable in the ongoing work of the HR function. Specifically, the activity involves the use of a systematic approach to decision making. Volumes of text have been written on the topic of decision making that include such methods as simple judgmental approaches to programmed approaches such as the program planning and budgeting system of the 1960s–1970s, and the earlier theoretical concepts set forth by Herbert Simon (1957), which focused on "organizations as kinds of institutionalized brains that fragment, routinize, and bound the decision-making process in order to make it manageable" (Morgan, 1986, p. 81).

We choose to view the organization/decision-making activity for HR purposes as *before* and *after* situations. That is, before the decision is made, the HR director and others must ask several key questions: (1) Is the matter at hand really a problem needing a decision? If so, what is the special problem that must be resolved? (2) Is the problem at hand within the "power" or authority of the HR unit to act? What other units and/or individuals necessarily should be involved in the decision-making process? (3) As HR director, am I or the involved group members willing to accept responsibility for solutions recommended? (4) What do we need to accomplish through the decision? (5) Are the relevant data/facts on hand and verified? (6) Are the internal and external environments ready for a decision on this matter? (7) Have the important logical decision options been identified, researched, and fully evaluated and assessed? (8) What are the possible impacts and/or ramifications of the various alternative solutions? (9) Which one solution best fits the case and fosters the best interests and needs of the school district's learners?

After the decision, other questions must be answered: (1) Has the recommended decision been reviewed with the appropriate school authorities and clearly communicated with appropriated internal and external groups and individuals? (2) What provisions have been made for implementation of the recommendation and later appropriate follow-up? (3) What specific evaluation and assessments will be implemented and by whom?

PARTICIPATING AND COOPERATIVE COLLABORATING ACTIVITIES

Virtually every model that has seen set forth for planning includes emphasis on participation and involvement of others. The concept of cooperative coordination was the main topic espoused by Mary Parker Follett in the early 1920s (Follett, 1924). She spoke of *integration* as the key to conflict resolution within organizations. Follett's (1940) four views of coordination were so revolutionary at the time that her collected papers were published by Metcalf and Urwick. The concept remains relevant today.

(1) Coordination by direct contact. Persons responsible for the work must be involved in organizational matters regardless of their position status, (2) Involvement/coordination must occur at the outset of policy formulation, not after the fact, (3) coordination must be viewed as a reciprocal relationship; existing relationships loom important, and (4) coordination must be viewed as a continuing process of individual and group communications.

"Participating involves cooperating with those affected for the best implementation, and collaborating is using all possible resources in order to achieve the best results. Each of these factors necessitates a knowledge and understanding of the system's internal and external environments". (Norton, 2008, p. 81)

MSG Experts (2016) underscored the importance of internal and external scanning in their statement that "environment must be scanned so as to determine development and forecast factors that will influence organizational success" (p. 1). They define *environmental scanning* as the possession and utilization of information about occasions, patterns, trends, and relationships within an organization's internal and external environment. Most every person in education is aware of the increasing competitiveness facing him or her regarding student enrollment, personnel recruitment and retention, financial support, and ongoing organizational changes.

"Environmental scanning refers to possession and utilization of information about patterns, trends, and relationships within an organization's internal and external environments. It helps the managers to decide the future path of the organization" (MSG Experts, 2016, p. 3). Scanning can reveal the opportunities and strengths of the HR function. It serves to help HR leaders: become more fully aware of school-community changes, identify the implications of political actions that are taking place and have effects on current HR activities, underscore critical needs for determining future program plans, avoid surprises, point out competitive actions and moves that influence operational effectiveness, and identify weaknesses that must be addressed in the HR programs and practices.

"Typically, the external scan focuses on emerging trends that present *opportunities* for the school district and potential *threats* to its continued effectiveness" (Norton, 2008, p. 87). Internal scanning focuses on the strengths and weaknesses of the school system that support or inhibit the school district's full potential. Without having such information in hand, school personnel leaders are operating in a vacuum. Both internal and external scans are activities that the human resources director can do with the cooperation of other local school leaders and various members of the school-community.

How do you find out about the strengths and weaknesses of the school system with a special focus on the human resources unit? You *ask the members* of the school staff and other community members that are especially active in school-community affairs. How do you find out about the *opportunities* or *threats* that the school and human resources function will encounter? You ask external organizations, research groups, local community agencies, and other influentials in the school community that might be part of the community power structure. The point is to be proactive rather than reactive in regard to meeting the tasks that you will face in the changing world of the human resources director.

WHO HAS THE EAR OF THE KING? A NOTE ON COMMUNITY POWER STRUCTURE

Historically, individuals and groups have been interested in the answer to the question, "Who has the ear of the king?" Previously in history, the ugly arena of politics was something that was to be avoided in education. Today, few people argue that education has no relation to the political world. In fact, education leaders today are well aware that education is fully a part of the political functions of government. Politics and the authoritative and legitimate distribution of valued resources are inextricably related to the everyday business of school leaders.

The concepts of internal and external scanning are facilitated by the extent to which the human resources director and other school district leaders are knowledgeable of the school community in which they work. Who are the people in the community who have much influence on what and how thing get done? As underscored by Morgan (1986), "power is the medium through which conflicts of interest are ultimately resolved. Power influences who gets what, when, and how" (p. 158). *Power structure* in a community commonly is described as being elite, factional, pluralistic, or inert. An elite power structure is one dominated by only 1% to 2% of the population. It receives little or no opposition.

School boards operating within an *elite power structure* commonly turn to one member for making a final decision; voting is always unanimous. On the other hand, a *factional* or *competitive power structure* is diffused, and the majority faction wins the day. *Pluralistic power* structures tend to be more open, and consensus is reached through discussion and diplomacy. An *inert* or *latent power structure* commonly depends on the status quo. In relation to school board actions, the school board generally depends on the school superintendent to make recommendations for its approval.

What does all of this have to do with the work of the human resources unit of the school district? The answer is "everything"! Human resources leaders can benefit by a knowledge of power sources in several ways. Leaders must be able to develop legitimate power bases themselves in order to deal effectively with the power bases within the school community. They must have the knowledge and ability to work with the school community and those persons who are in positions to influence that impact on personnel policies and regulations. Without such ability, the HR director is in a reactive rather than a proactive position to lead.

Several years ago, perhaps Leslie Kindred (1957) said it best: "Effective planning depends upon a thorough understanding of the setting in which the plan takes place. . . .. It must start with a factual knowledge of people in the community and how they live. The more that is known about them, the better are the chances for establishing successful communication" (p. 39). One procedure for getting to know the school community is to meet and visit with various community members who are directly involved and therefore knowledgeable of policy making and how decisions are made or not made in the community.

Norton (1968) wrote about ways to get to know your school community in ten easy lessons. These recommendations are as follows:

(1) As a human resources director, visit with the school superintendent as well as members of the school board. The board will consist of members commonly representative of several aspects of the community.

(2) Confer with the local manager of the Chamber of Commerce or local prominent business person. These individuals will have had many contacts with the various "publics" of the school community.

(3) Arrange to visit with members of the city council or other officials such as the city manager.

(4) Visit with the president of the several civic clubs that exist in the community. They work directly with a variety of members who are interested and involved in a variety of community projects.

(5) Arrange a visit with the editor(s) of the local newspaper. Editors are likely to be aware of the real community issues and concerns.

(6) Arrange a special visit with the chief administrative assistants within your school district, the business manager, athletic director, head custodian, and others. Attempt to gain their viewpoints on the publics that they encounter in the fulfillment of their duties.

(7) Ask the local parent-teacher association for thirty minutes at their next planning meeting. Emphasize your interest in gaining their views of the community and its educational objectives.

(8) Decide to visit with the president of the teachers' association of the school district or other teacher committee appropriate for your purpose. Focus on their ideas and suggestions for improving the personnel function of the school district.

(9) Arrange to visit with two or three human resources directors of other business and industrial organizations in the community. Focus on two or three of the most important questions/problems/practices that are facing them and how they are meeting the ongoing changes.

(10) While other publics, groups, agencies, and groups/individuals in the school community perhaps should be contacted, you already have enough information to provide valuable help in your work as human resources director. Spend sufficient time to reflect on your visits and the information gained. What are the implications for your leadership in the role?

We suspect that some of you are saying to yourself, "We wouldn't be able to do those things in our school district. Only the school superintendent or public relations director can speak to community persons on school matters." There seems to be some concern that someone will say something publicly that becomes a problem or is his or her idea but not the "voice" of the school board. We submit that this is a major mistake of public communication. If leaders in the HR office of the school district are not in a position to visit with other bodies and individuals within the school community, what makes them competent to act as the human resources leader?

In fact, it has been shown that the school's publics want to hear more from other leaders of the school district's programs, the teachers, the school principals, the personnel directors, and others in levels of authority within the school district. And, some member of the school community would favor less communication from the school superintendent and his or her designated "spokesperson." Participating and collaborating activities demand the involvement of the significant others that are leading important aspects of the school district's programs.

PLANNING VERSUS THE PLAN

Planning is a comprehensive, continuous process that is characterized by flexibility and responsiveness to change. It centers on the formation of a strategy or program for the accomplishment of desired outcomes. . . . A plan is a product of the planning process; it is a fixed entity that is time and place specific (Norton, 2008, p. 79).

The success of your planning activities rests on the extent to which the plan(s) enhance the value and effectiveness of your program outcomes. Was the school district's recruitment process improved? Were the retention rates of personnel improved? Did the planned program of personnel growth and development result in improved employee practices? Did you do your best to communicate the positive results in terms of hard data? What hard data can be presented to support the added value of the planning process?

Although qualitative results can serve to illustrate accountability results, school boards commonly are interested in cost figures. How did the planning activities and the plan result in added value in terms of dollars and cents? The crux of the evaluation of your human resources plan is vested in the extent to which it added to the value of the school district's strategic plan and to the goals of the human resources function.

ORGANIZATIONAL DEVELOPMENT: TO ACCOMPLISH MORE SUCCESSFUL CHANGE AND HUMAN PERFORMANCE

Check each of the following entries that you believe are important objectives of the school district's human resources function:

1. To increase the level of interpersonal trust among employees.____
2. To increase employees' level of satisfaction and commitment.____
3. To confront problems instead of neglecting them.____
4. To manage conflict effectively. ____
5. To increase cooperation and collaboration among the employees.____

6. To increase the organization's problem-solving capacity._____
7. To put in place processes that will help improve the ongoing operation of the organization on a continuous basis. _____

Everyone might check each of the seven entries as ones that relate directly to the objectives of the human resources function. The catch is that the seven entries are viewed as the objectives of organizational development (OD). *Organizational development* is commonly defined as "a body of knowledge and practice that enhances organizational performance and individual development, by increasing alignment among various systems within the overall system. OD interventions are inclusive methodological approaches to strategic planning, organization design, leadership development, change management, performance management, coaching, team building, and work balance" (Minahan [Organizational Development Network], 2016, p. 1).

The Organizational Development Network goes on to say that all organizational development programs try to achieve the following objectives:

1. Making individuals in the organization aware of the vision of the organization. Organizational development helps in making employees align with the vision of the organization.
2. Encouraging employees to solve problems instead of avoiding them.
3. Strengthening interpersonal trust, cooperation, and communication for the successful achievement of organizational goals.
4. Encouraging every individual to participate in the process of planning, thus making that individual feel responsible for the implementation of the plan.
5. Creating a work atmosphere in which employees are encouraged to work and participate enthusiastically.
6. Replacing lines of authority with personal knowledge and skill.
7. Creating an environment of trust so that employees willingly accept change.

It will not be possible to include each of the foregoing objectives/values in this chapter; however, the following discussions will include the important human resources objectives related to the development of trust in the school system, managing conflict, aligning the work of the HR function with the overall vision of the school district, creating a positive and open climate within the school district, and increasing employee job satisfaction and commitment. Each of these topics serves to underscore the primary OD responsibilities and contributions of the HR function within the school district.

PRE-QUIZ

Take a few minutes to complete the following true or false pre-quiz. Don't just guess the answer; rather, if you are not sure about an answer, just move on to the next question. Your score and a discussion of each of the ten questions follow the quiz.

1. Although much has been written about school climate, there has yet to be available sufficient research to support climate and its effects on student achievement. ____True or ____False
2. The terms *climate* and *culture* are synonymous and used interchangeably in education. ____True or ____False
3. Trust is similar to the weather; there is much talk about it, but in reality there isn't much that one can do about it. Either you have trust or you don't. ____True or ____False
4. Conflict is a common problem facing HR leaders, but little or no research is available for dealing with it. ____True or ____False
5. School goals and objectives to be effective must center on the single program, school unit, or school function in question. That is, a function such as human resources must set its goals and objectives on its own views of what is to be accomplished. ____True or ____False
6. Job satisfaction has been studied historically with the constant finding that positive job satisfaction and employee commitment are affected overwhelmingly by the level of monetary compensation received. ____True or ____False
7. Teacher workload in schools nationally has been found generally to be "fair and equitable" as shown by the fact that most every school requires a teaching load of four or five classes daily. ____True or ____False
8. Controversy in an open climate can be useful. ____True or ____False
9. Trust comes from the human resources director's ability to set forth a vision of what he or she plans to accomplish for employees. ____True or ____False
10. Organizational development, as it relates to the work of the HR director, includes putting in place processes that will serve to improve the effectiveness of the HR function on a continuous basis. ____True or ____False

Answers to the Pre-Quiz

Question 1 is false, question 2 is false, question 3 is false, question 4 is false, question 5 is false, question 6 is false, question 7 is false, question 8 is true, question 9 is false, question 10 is true.

Scoring Results

Your Score

9–10 correct—five stars*****
7–8 correct—four stars****
5–6 correct—three stars***
3–4 correct—two stars**
1–2 correct—one star*
0 correct—out of stars

Discussion of the Pre-Quiz

1. Question 1, "There has yet to be available sufficient research to support climate and its effects on student achievement," is false. Since the early 1960s, much attention has been given to the topic of school climate and to the culture of the school. Although these concepts have similarities, they are quite different in many respects. Each study tends to find similar results: a positive school climate has important positive effects on student achievement, decreased student dropout rates, reduced student discipline problems, increased attitude toward learning, and creativity and innovation among the instructional staff.

   HR directors work cooperatively with school principals in fostering positive school climate for several reasons: cooperating with principals and others in setting a set of shared goals and objectives for professional and classified personnel, providing a wide variety of activities for personnel growth and improvement, recommending personnel policies and establishing administrative procedures in relation to personnel administration, and establishing an effective program for retaining highly qualified personnel for service in the school district.

2. Question 2, "The terms *culture* and *climate* are synonymous," is false. It is true that the terms *culture* and *climate* have similarities; nevertheless, they are different concepts. The similarities include the fact that both have people as the primary concern and both are based on shared goals and interpersonal relationships. Socialization is a common characteristic, and environmental factors are important to each concept. Traditions and artifact are of interest to both climate and culture.

   However, the concept of *culture* is more normative than climate since it centers on the values, belief, customs, and underlying assumptions of members across an array of dimensions that go beyond the concept of personal relationships. Morgan (1986) argues that culture is something that is never easily changed, if at all. Organizational cultures are deeply engrained values, belief, traditions, and attitudes that go much deeper than merely improving interpersonal relationships.

Climate, on the other hand, is viewed as the collective personality of the school or school system. It is more interpersonal and revealed in the attitudes and behaviors of school personnel and community members. Climate is more focused on the process and condition of the school member's life, such as job satisfaction, friendly relationships, cooperative attitudes, and equality of staff treatment.

3. Question 3, "Trust is similar to the weather. . ... Either you have trust or you don't," is false. Hoy and Tschannen-Moran (1999) set forth the concept that *trust* is a person's willingness to be vulnerable to another person on the basis of confidence that the latter person is *benevolent, reliable, competent, honest*, and *open*.

Three examples follow: (1) Honesty is the truthfulness, integrity, and authenticity of a person or group. Trusted administrators reveal a consistency between words and actions. They accept responsibility for their actions rather than distorting the truth by shifting the blame elsewhere. (2) At the most basic level, trust has to do with the predictability that is consistently in knowing what to expect from others. Reliability is confidence that others will consistently act in ways that are beneficial to the trustee. (3) Openness is giving of oneself. Openness breeds trust just as trust breeds openness. Your personal wisdom doesn't magically rise to the top when you become principal or human resources director. You realistically will not have all the right answers. When faced with a question for which you do not have the answer, it's best to admit the fact but agree to work with the person(s) to find out the best answer to the question.

Administrators in closed climates engender mistrust by unsuccessful attempts to spin the truth to make their view of reality the accepted standard. In open climates, mistakes are freely admitted and addressed rather than hidden and ignored. On one occasion, a high school teacher commented that "one never knows where they stand with the school principal; there is never one-on-one conversations." Trust is facilitated when face-to-face, personal contacts are practiced.

When HR leaders address each of the several facets of trust listed above, the end results will be evidenced in the school district's climate and in the achievement levels of students and all other school personnel. Trust serves to expedite important outcomes, including positive relationships, effective communication, positive motivation, and achievement of the school district's goals and objectives.

4. Question 4, "Conflict is a common problem facing HR leaders, but little or no research is available for dealing with it," is false. The study of

organizational conflict has been a topic of concern historically. In 1924, Mary Parker Follett set forth her concept of integration for resolving conflicts that inevitably occur in all organizations. *Integration* is when two parties are brought together for sharing their ideas on a matter based upon the facts of the case.

The ideas are integrated and ultimately become united in pursuit of a common goal (Norton, 2008). The win-win results permit both parties to realize their goals to the greatest extent possible. Follett's concepts of depersonalization contended that each person involved in a matter of conflict must take his or her orders from the situation. That is, persons involved in the situation must set aside their personal interests and give thought to what is best for achieving the important goals of the organization. In resolving conflict, consider the following strategies:

(1) Take action on the conflict situation at the very first opportunity; the longer the conflict is present, the more difficult it is to resolve. (2) Gathering and understanding the facts surrounding the situation can do much to reduce undue criticism since it serves to identify constructive and destructive proposals. (3) Work to understand the values held by each party of the conflict situation and help them look professionally at the values that best serve the purposes of the school system. (4) Realize that conflict in every kind of school system is bound to occur; in fact, criticism can be useful in underscoring the existing issues within the school system and ones that must be resolved for the betterment of all concerned. (5) Maintain both personal integrity and the integrity of the school system. A positive approach to such matters can result in better solutions to existing problems.

5. Question 5, "A function such as human resources must set its goals and objectives on its own views of what is to be accomplished," is false. The environmental scanning completed by the school district provides important information that affects the strategic and operational planning for the school system overall. From this basis, operational plans are developed for each school unit in relation to budgeting, personnel, pupil services, and other administrative activities. In turn, school system operational plans are developed for other major district areas, such as pupil personnel services, financing and business affairs, and human resources. The operational plan for the human resources unit is tied closely not only to the school district's strategic plan but also to other system units, such as schools, departments, and divisions. The term *system* conveys the concepts presented herein.

Likert (1967) recommended *a linking-pin concept* to ensure horizontal and vertical communication/relationships within the system. Each unit in the system is organized so that a member of any one unit is also a member of another unit so that he or she could serve as a link between a primary unit and another unit for communication/relationship purposes. It is common for the human resources director to work closely with the director of instructional services or business services. In any case, we give special emphasis to the importance having the HR director having a seat at the table of the school superintendent's administrative cabinet.

6. Question 6, "Job satisfaction has been studied historically with the constant finding that positive job satisfaction and employee commitment are affected overwhelmingly by the level of monetary compensation received," is false. Historically, research studies have revealed that employee and supervisor relations are more important for job satisfaction than monetary considerations. An early study by Herzberg et al. (1959) considered the factors that lead to job satisfaction and job dissatisfaction. Later, such factors for teachers and administrators were studied. The factors that led to job satisfaction for teachers in rank order were as follows: (1) achievement, (2) recognition, (3) work itself, and (4) responsibility. Salary was not mentioned as a factor in the top four of the list. Factors that brought about job dissatisfaction for teachers were as follows: (1) interpersonal relations with students, (2) interpersonal relations with peers, (3) company policy and administration, and (4) technical supervision. Salary/compensation was not listed by administrators as one of the top four reasons for job satisfaction or job dissatisfaction.

   However, more recent studies in the areas of business and industry have revealed that benefits and salary have moved toward the top of the list as factors of job satisfaction and engagement. Additional research on this topic would be beneficial for personnel employed in education.

7. Question 7, "Teacher workload in schools nationally has been found generally to be 'fair and equitable,'" is false. Teacher workload studies have made it clear that inequities are inhibiting the performance of many of the school's best teachers. It is common for teacher load indices to differ widely within a school's staff. In some load studies, it has been found that a teacher is carrying a teacher load two or even three times that of a teacher in the same school with the lowest teacher load. In addition, new teachers commonly carry the highest teacher load indices among the school teacher personnel.

   We have procedures for measuring the load of the school teacher that result in a statistic that can be used to examine inequities in load assignments. The practice of having teachers teach the same number of classes each day is accepted as the equitable way to assign teacher duties. We submit that the HR director holds the responsibility of cooperating with the school principal to determine equitable teacher load assignments. Many factors besides the number of classes taught serve to make up the total load of the teacher. If such inequities are not known and not resolved by the school principal, the school's best teachers most likely will become overburdened and their teaching performance even reduced to a level of mediocrity.

8. Question 8, "Controversy in an open climate can be useful," is true. "In a healthy school climate, the consideration of controversial matters can be useful. Progress in terms of goal achievement and new understandings is often generated through opportunities to reflect on problems and alternative solutions" (Norton, 2008, p. 247).

9. Question 9, "Trust comes from the human resources director's ability to set forth a vision of what he or she plans to accomplish for employees," is false. Several important needs are vital in building trust among the school staff. First of all, the HR leader must make every effort to accomplish the interests of the school personnel. Just expressing these interests is not enough; they must demonstrate that the interests of the personnel are being attended. The implementation of the employees' interests is crucial; good intentions will not suffice to produce trust. HR directors build trust by demonstrating actions that they have espoused regarding what actions will be taken and accepting the responsibility for the results.

10. Question 10, "Organizational development, as it relates to the work of the HR director, includes putting in place processes that will serve to improve the effectiveness of the HR function on a continuous basis," is true. Improving the climate within the school district, dealing effectively with business and financial practices, establishing effective communication among the school personnel and within the school community, coordinating the many processes of the HR function with other units within the school system, building employee trust, and planning strategically in tune with the overall school system are vital organizational development activities of the HR director's office.

SELF-EVALUATION CHECKLIST FOR CHAPTER 2

We consider this chapter on the topic of planning and organization as one of the most important chapters of the book. First, it serves as the foundation for fostering effective programs and practices for the human resources function. Second, we find that all too often planning is viewed as a periodic meeting of the HR director and other members of the school district's staff. Third, effective planning is ongoing and specifically focused on in-depth strategies and research-based information. And, last, we find knowledge of the important processes of forecasting, designing, and strategizing to be generally lacking in the overall activities of the HR function. Proactive strategies in these areas are essential.

SELF-EVALUATION QUIZ CHECKLIST
FOR LEADERSHIP IN PLANNING

We provide a pre-summary of this chapter by asking you to take the following self-evaluation assessment on leadership in planning. For each entry, circle the level of skill/knowledge that you presently possess. Second, check the level of skill/knowledge that is actually needed in the position of HR director. The results are for personal edification; no other person needs to know the results. Do your best to be as objective in your responses; you are the benefactor in this case. The response of (F) *familiarity* suggests that you are able to discuss the nature of the entry, *understanding* (U) infers that you are able to explain the techniques associated with the entry, and (A) *application* suggests that you are able to perform and/or demonstrate the related procedures/strategies related to the entry.

Type of Knowledge/Skill	Your Present Level of Performance			Performance Level Needed		
Forecasting Techniques	F	U	A	F	U	A
Environmental Scanning	F	U	A	F	U	A
Planning Leadership	F	U	A	F	U	A
Climate Measures	F	U	A	F	U	A
Conflict Management	F	U	A	F	U	A
Job Satisfaction Assessment	F	U	A	F	U	A
Strategic Planning Methods	F	U	A	F	U	A
Organizational Design	F	U	A	F	U	A
Leadership Development	F	U	A	F	U	A
Change Management	F	U	A	F	U	A
Performance Management	F	U	A	F	U	A
Team Building	F	U	A	F	U	A
Coaching/Mentoring	F	U	A	F	U	A
Work-Life Balance Measures	F	U	A	F	U	A
Problem-Solving Strategies	F	U	A	F	U	A
Data Collection Procedures	F	U	A	F	U	A
Group Process Facilitation	F	U	A	F	U	A
Human Relations Skills	F	U	A	F	U	A
Inter-unit Coordination	F	U	A	F	U	A
School-Community Relations	F	U	A	F	U	A
Budgeting/Fiscal Management	F	U	A	F	U	A

By examining your responses in the foregoing checklist, you can identify what you perceive as your strengths, ones that you already have in place. Most everyone has areas in which his or her knowledge and skills are not as strong as they need to be. First of all, keep giving emphasis to your strengths.

As noted by Clifton and Nelson (1992), people soar with their strengths. That is, you will improve additionally and be more effective by emphasizing your strengths than giving the majority of time to improving areas of weakness. You might see it as important to select one or two areas of "weakness" to improve, especially the area that is a crucial component of your work.

We submit that staff development is self-development. Improvement is a personal matter; Your self-image is the primary motivator for determining what incentives will serve to encourage the effectiveness of your personal individual development plan. Real growth begins when the individual assumes the major responsibility for his or her own professional growth. This is not to imply that personal development does not need the support of others, but effective growth is mainly intrinsic and "forced" involvement in mandated in-service programs will likely be revealed in ineffective, short-lived results.

A key fact for you to remember is that the largest single factor driving job satisfaction is the opportunity for growth and career development (Bathhurst, 2007). Empirical studies have revealed that if a wide variety of growth activities are not available in the organization, quality personnel will seek other options of employment.

WHAT EFFECTIVE PLANNING IS AND WHAT IT IS NOT

Sometimes, it helps to define a concept by not only telling what it is but by examining what it is not. Table 2.3 summarizes several characteristics of effective planning and also underscores what effective planning is not. Norton (2008) defined the term *planning* as "the comprehensive continuous process that is characterized by flexibility and responsiveness to change. It centers on the formation of a strategy or program for the accomplishment of desired outcomes" (p. 79).

Key Chapter Ideas and Recommendations

- Planning and organizational processes are foundational to all other processes of the HR function. It is of utmost importance that the HR director understands the important differences concerning what effective HR planning/organization is and what it is not.
- HR planning includes several key components that must be addressed: forecasting, designing, strategizing, organizing, cooperating, and collaborating.
- Planning and the plan are different entities. Planning is a comprehensive, continuous process that is characterized by flexibility within an environment of ongoing change. A plan is the outcome of the planning process.

Table 2.3.   Effective HR Planning

Effective HR Planning Is	*Effective HR Planning Is Not*
A systematic way of determining goals and objectives for the HR function	Merely a reaction to immediate problems and needs facing the HR function
A process for viewing the visions of the HR unit's future	Simply the writing of a plan of action
A strategy for establishing priorities for the HR function's mission	A brainstorming meeting scheduled by the HR director to personnel to discuss what the group wants to do for a specified period of time
Scheduled evaluation and assessment	A reporting session for weighing the problems being encountered in the area of employee job activities
Sessions for examining collected information and data relative to the progress being made toward the goals and objectives set forth in the HR function's strategic plan	
A strategy set forth for implementation with specific procedures relative to purposes, schedules, assignments, responsibilities, and specific resources/financial support	Simply a statement of what should be done by someone sometime or what is needed to be done
A specific procedure for involving appropriate personnel in the primary decision-making process	An activity statement of what the HR central office will be doing and what it is expected to do relative to the educational programs activities of the HR function
An important strategic process for anticipating the changes within the school community that must be anticipated and considered for continued program improvement	A meeting of the minds relative to what changes we want to make in our program of personnel management
An ongoing humanistic process that provides the HR director, administrative staff, school board and school community an opportunity to monitor, assess, evaluate, and change the HR program's effectiveness	A singular process that focuses on the specific goals and objectives of the HR central office

- The costs of employee turnover militate against the stability of the school system. Employee turnover for any reason is detrimental to school purposes. Employee retention is just as important as employee recruitment.
- The knowledge and skills relative to such planning components as forecasting must be addressed by any individual that assumes the leadership of the HR function in the school system.

- Schools operate within the culture and the climate of the school community. Each of these phenomena has major effects on the goals of the HR function. Internal and external scanning strategies must be in place and utilized when establishing HR program practices.
- The adage of "know the community" looms important for HR directors. Community outreach must be extended in order that HR goals and goals and objectives are accomplished.
- All organizations will encounter conflict. The HR director and other school leaders must be knowledgeable and skilled in methods and strategies in the area of conflict resolution.
- Planning and organization, as it relates to the HR function, must give major attention to how these processes tie strategically to the overall goals and purposes of the school district and other units within the district.
- Empirical and basic research results have revealed major inequities in teacher workload assignments. Attention to the matter of teacher workload has been neglected historically in education. As a result, the negative outcomes of workload inequities continue. Unless HR directors and school principal become skilled and knowledgeable in the area of teacher workload and assessment strategies, teacher retention and inequitable work assignments will continue to be problematic in schools nationally.

DISCUSSION QUESTIONS

1. This chapter emphasized the importance of planning components, such as forecasting. Forecasting requires special knowledge and skills relating to data collection and analysis. Both time and resources are required. However, give thought to the results of not gaining such information. What are the probable outcomes on both personnel and financial matters?
2. You, as HR director of the school system, are speaking to a representative body of community members. At one point you mention the term *OD activities*. A hand goes up in the audience and the individual asks the question, "What do you mean by OD activities?" What is your reply?
3. As director of the human resources function for the school district, you are speaking to officers of the local teachers' association on the topic of teacher rights. During the questioning period, one teacher asks, "Who is responsible in the school district for assigning the workload of teachers?" She goes on to say that "I know the school principal has certain responsibilities in this regard, but we get requests from several other sources such as the human resources office, curriculum director's office, and other central office personnel. How are the teacher load assignments considered from a fair and equitable point of view? Isn't there some way to determine

workloads and deal with the many inequities that presently are occurring?" How will you respond?

4. Differentiate between the terms *school culture* and *school climate*. We often hear someone say that "we need to change the culture of the school." In view of the information set forth in this chapter on the topic of climate and culture, what might be your response or explanation to the comment?

CASE 2.1 WHY GO TO ALL THAT WORK?

Andrew Scott had just been named to the position of human resources director for the Lafayette School District. He is from another state and was selected from among several position candidates as being especially effective in the matters of strategic planning. When interviewed by the school superintendent, Merlin George, Scott had explained his *model* for working closely with the school community and relationships with the teachers' association in his previous position.

During the first week of Scott's service with Lafayette, the topic of strategic planning was brought to the table.

"A priority for the human resources unit," said Superintendent George, "is to develop an HR plan that ties strategically to the school district's strategic plan and you need to . . ."

"Oh," interrupted Scott, "I have that matter well in hand. You will recall the plan that I described during the interview process. I plan to use the strategic plan that I put together for my former school district. It has all the bells and whistles that are needed and should be easily implemented in our human resources program here at Lafayette."

Discussion Exercise

In view of the information on strategic planning set forth in this chapter, what should be Superintendent George's response in this case? Assume the role of Superintendent George and draft a paragraph that represents your specific comments to Andrew Scott relative to his recommendation.

REFERENCES

Bathhurst, P. (2007, March 11). Training is the key at top firms. *Arizona Republic*, p. ED1.

Clifton, D. O., & Nelson, P. (1992). *Soar with your strengths*. New York: Dell.

Follett, M. P. (1924). *Creative experience*. New York: Longmans, Green.

Follett, M.P. (1940). The meaning of responsibility in business management. In H.C. Metcalf & L. Urwick (Eds.), *Dynamic administration: The collected papers of Mary Parker Follett* (pp. 146–166). New York: Harper & Brothers.

Herzberg, F., Mausner, B., & Snyderman, B. (1959). *The motivation to work.* New York: Wiley.

Hoy, W., & Tschannen-Moran, M. (1999). The five faces of trust: An empirical confirmation in urban elementary schools. *Journal of School Leadership, 9,* 184–208.

Kindred, L.L. (1957). *School public relations.* Englewood Cliffs, NJ: Prentice-Hall.

Likert, R. (1967). *The human organization.* New York: McGraw-Hill.

Minahan, M. MM & Associates (2016, April 26). *What is organizational development.* Silver Springs, MD: Author.

Morgan, G. (1986). *Images of organization.* Newbury Park, CA: Sage.

MSG Experts (2016, April 23). *Environmental scanning—Internal & external analysis of environment.* From the Web: http://managementstudyguide.com/envionmental-scznning.htm

Norton, M.S. (1968, January). *Know your community in ten easy lessons. The Clearing House.* Teaneck, NJ: Fairleigh Dickinson University Press.

Norton, M. S. (2008). *Human resources administration for educational leaders.* Thousand Oaks, CA: Sage.

Simon, H. (1957). *Administrative behavior* (2nd ed.). New York: Macmillan.

Smith, R.E. (2005). *Human resources administration: A school-based perspective.* Larchmont, NY: Eye on Education.

Chapter 3

Staffing the Schools for Educational and Support Services

Primary chapter goal: To set forth guidelines for implementing the primary human resources processes of personnel recruitment, re-recruitment, and hiring of professional and classified staff employees for the school district.

OUR LAMENT

America has yet to face seriously the facts of teacher supply, teacher recruitment, quality teachers, teacher compensation, and teacher retention. Yes, we have talked a great deal about these matters, but little or nothing much has been done to change these conditions. A large majority of American citizens would place education at the top of the list of national priorities. Yet, governmental and local expenditures for various programs, services, and commodities have not reflected this priority. Historically, Americans spend an estimated two-and-a-half times more on alcohol beverages alone than on education annually.

When great teachers do enter the teaching profession, reportedly they are among the ones that are not retained after the first year of teaching. Doesn't the best education in the world for children and youth need the best school leaders, teachers, and support personnel that provide and support student learning experiences? America will not achieve this worthy goal until the time its people support what they say: "education is America's highest priority."

It should be noted that the human resources function in some quarters has been referred to as IR, the *inhuman resources* function. The reference is speaking most directly to incidences of employee mishandling. This fact indeed is unfortunate. To be objective in relation to the effectiveness of human resources practices, a word about its ineffectiveness is in order. Visits with practicing HR directors do result in learning about certain shortcomings of the HR function. Perhaps empirical research findings relative to the HR director's preparation for the position are a case in point.

Few HR directors express the fact that they were well prepared to assume the position of human resources director. Some directors have taken a course in their graduate program on personnel administration. All too often, the activities that are being practiced in the role are ones that are learned on the job. On-the-job learning generally means the continuation of marginal or "less than the best" practices. The common preparation pursuit for practicing HR directors is the completion of a master's degree in educational administration with only three semester hours of a thirty-six-credit-hour degree program devoted to personnel administration. Very few persons that enter a degree program in educational administration do so with the intent to "major" in human resources administration.

One study found that six of ten HR directors presently in the position did not plan to remain in the role as a professional career. Empirical evidence suggests that approximately one-third of the practicing HR directors are in their first three years of service (Norton, 2009). It is true that many universities nationally offer programs that focus on human resources management. These programs commonly are available in the business colleges rather than colleges of education and tend to emphasize personnel practices in business and industrial organizations.

Quality preparation for human resources administration remains lacking in higher education programs. In an earlier study, approximately two-thirds of the directors judged themselves as being only "fairly well prepared" to assume the HR director's position and 20% reported being "not well prepared." A recommended preparation program for human resources directors is presented later in this chapter.

The important HR processes of job analysis and the designing of job prescriptions have, for the most part, been outsourced to school board associations and other external job offices. One HR director in a middle-sized city did not have a position description for the position that he held. In that school district, it can be assumed that all of the known benefits of implementing job analysis and preparing job descriptions for the school district and its employees are lost. Poor human resources operations result when poor practices in inhuman resources administration are evident.

The lack of data regarding the results of HR practices, the lack of attention given to valid personnel research findings, the use of boilerplate job descriptions and personnel policies, the lack of quality preparation programs for the work required in an effective HR program, and the lip service attention that is all too often given to meeting the real interests and needs of the school personnel are all factors that contribute to *employee mishandling* within the school district.

PLANNING IS ALL INVASIVE

Effective human resources leaders initiate program improvements and creative strategies for achieving them; they are proactive as opposed to being reactive. Once the HR director sees the need for positive change, he or she takes steps to initiate it. As chapter 2 emphasizes, planning in all its aspects comes into being. Consideration is given to the return on investment. A worthy idea remains stagnant until it is supported by funding and related human resources. Thus, marketing the program change looms important.

Your marketing strategies depend largely on the effectiveness of soliciting the cooperation of the school personnel. Do your best to make the new plan that of the employees. Keep an accurate account of the outcomes of the program changes in question. Report outcomes accurately and make adjustments that focus on the positive factors of the program changes. Give credit for favorable results as it is due. Let other school leaders and the school district's board of education know how their support has been a factor in the program's success.

CHAPTER SNAPSHOT—BIGGEST PROBLEM FOR PUBLIC EDUCATION? LACK OF FUNDING, POLL SAYS

Dylan Scott (2012, May 12) reported the following information from a Gallup poll that focused directly on the matter at hand. "Americans believe a lack of financial support is the biggest problem currently facing public schools, according to the 44th annual Phi Delta Kappa International/Gallup poll of public attitudes toward public schools released . . . but they also say that balancing the budget is more important than improving the quality of education."

Funding was by far the most pegged problem in the poll, with 35% of those polled saying it is the biggest obstacle for public schools in their community. At the same time, however, 60% said it is more important for the federal government to balance its checkbook over the next five years than to improve the quality of public education, which earned 38% of the votes polled (Scott, 2012).

It does seem to be of major importance to keep in mind that the federal government presently provides approximately 10% of the funds in support of public education. States and local communities provide the remaining 90%. In addition, approximately 52% of those persons polled agreed with the concept of including standardized test scores in teacher evaluations, 57% believed that entrance requirements for college teacher preparation programs should be more rigorous, and 33% expressed the opinion that such a change would result in more effective teachers.

We tend to agree with the latter opinion of more rigorous entrance requirements for college teacher preparation programs but would argue for an attractive scholarship/loan program to accompany the higher preparation requirements along with a provision of a 25% loan reduction for each year that the graduated teacher serves in the classroom following graduation and licensure. However, we submit that the idea of using student test results for evaluating teaching performance is flawed and should not be practiced. Our reasoning is set forth in the following section of the chapter.

RE-RECRUITMENT: AN ONGOING PROCESS OF PRIMARY IMPORTANCE

Re-recruitment is vested in the efforts of the human resources director and other school leaders to retain qualified personnel in the school system. Teacher turnover has been consistently high historically, and so today a loss of one-third of first-year teachers each year has become viewed as "normal." Employee retention is one of the most critical issues facing human resources leaders, including school principals.

We question as to whether human resources directors ever take a course on retaining quality personnel. Re-recruitment is especially important today since the competition for talented personnel is highly competitive. Nevertheless, the concepts and procedures discussed in relation to professional employees will apply as well for the school district's classified personnel.

At the elementary school level, we hire teachers to teach grades 1 through 6. In departmentalized secondary schools, we hire teachers who have specialized in a variety of subject matter areas. But how about the hiring of classified personnel? Isn't the hiring focused primarily on secretarial staff, maintenance/facility workers, and food service personnel? Not quite!

Take, for example, the job family of maintenance and facility workers. One school system in California listed the following job titles under the job family of maintenance and facility workers: carpenter, head custodian, custodian, electrician, electrician assistant, electronics repair worker, field maintenance groundskeeper, furniture repair worker, gardener, gardener tree topper, locksmith, locksmith assistant, office machines repair, painter, painter assistant, heating and ventilation mechanic, journeyman plumber, roofer, and sheet metal worker.

The problems of hiring and then retaining certificated personnel relate equally well to classified employees. We must keep in mind that classified personnel commonly constitute 30% to 50% of the total personnel of the school district staff. In a school district with a student enrollment of 28,000 students and a pupil-teacher ratio of 20 to 1, the school district would need to employ 1,400 teachers. If we assume that the 1,400 teachers represent 70% of the total school staff, the classified staff would approximate 600 employees.

Classified personnel commonly belong to many different job families, such as office, maintenance, food, custodial, transportation, technical, buildings and grounds, para-educators, and security.

Qualified personnel in the foregoing classifications are recruited by most every business and industry in operation. Retaining qualified personnel in these positions is similar to the problems of retaining certificated staff. As one director of classified personnel lamented, "it seems that just when we hire and spend time and money training classified personnel, they find another job outside education with higher compensation and often more attractive fringe benefits." Chapter 5 discusses the topic of classified personnel in-depth.

KEEPING THE GOOD PEOPLE

Re-recruitment, also termed *strategic staffing*, is the extended efforts by the human resources director, school principal, and others to retain effective personnel in the school or school system. It is not a special effort toward the time of retirement to take steps for retaining a teacher, administrator, or classified staff employee to withhold retirement for a year or more. Rather, re-recruitment begins immediately upon hiring and continues as long as the employee is serving the school district toward the accomplishment of its goals and objectives. Thus, teacher placement, orientation activities, work-life balance considerations, professional development opportunities, job satisfaction, and other actions that center on the employee's interests and needs loom important in the re-recruitment process.

Berglas (1973), Lemke (1995), and Mahoney (2006) have underscored the importance of giving early attention to the process of re-recruitment. Berglas's study found that an early induction program that especially provides personal assistance is the single best factor of all morale factors for personnel new to the school system. Lemke reported that meaningful orientation programs for personnel new to the school system raised retention rates from 50% to 85%. Such findings should start the program implementation wheels turning immediately.

Mahoney noted that effective induction programs help in bonding the employees to the school and school system, leading them to the conclusion that they are an important member of the school system's team. Such orientation activities must be extended into a continuous program of professional development activities that address the employee's personal interests and strengths. If such provisions are not available, quality personnel tend to seek employment elsewhere.

GIVING ATTENTION TO RE-RECRUITMENT

Robinson and Galpin (1996) set forth a brief but significant list of relationship practices for HR leaders as they focus on re-recruitment. The following considerations are based on these authors' concepts for re-recruitment leadership.

1. Protection (assurance, surety, certainty, safety, confidence, stability, integration, security)—The employee must come to believe that he or she is an important member of the school and school system's team and that the mission of the school system cannot be fully accomplished without his or her continued contributions.
2. Participation (involved, collaborative, sharing, related, inclusion)—Employees are able to be in on things and be a respected part of the decision-making process. Employees know that they can ask, question, recommend, and take responsibility.
3. Autonomy (direction, regulate, guide, assurance, self-assurance, control)—Creative people want to be able to use their own talents in ways that create important outcomes. They are willing to be held accountable but want to be able to have a primary input into how the work is accomplished.
4. Self-esteem (self-importance, self-worth, I, ego)—The feeling or belief that the employee truly plays an important role in the accomplishment of stated purposes must be based on the genuine behaviors of the school leaders and communicated both in their behavior and communication.
5. Competency—(knowledge, skill, requisite ability, qualified, successful, effective decision maker)—Leader(s) reveal skill in effective decision making and communicating with personnel relative to the underlying rationale and importance for needed changes in organizational programs and practices.

A planned ongoing program for employee retention between the HR director and local school principals is necessary for implementing various retention activities. How do school administrators learn of employees' personal attitudes and interests? They ask them! In some cases, a sincere verbal comment regarding an employee's behavior looms important.

A PROACTIVE WAY TO KNOW YOUR STAFF

I recommend the use of a personal interest questionnaire at least twice a year as a retention activity. Although person-to-person discussions reportedly serve the best purpose, a one-page feedback check also can be a viable feedback tool. Figure 3.1 is an example of a personal interest questionnaire. It commonly is administered by the school principal in cooperation with the school district's HR director.

Effective re-recruitment activities have several key characteristics. Such activities must be ongoing and sincere. Manipulative efforts are not effective; motivating efforts tend to release employee efforts. Such efforts are revealed in activities that result in employee appreciation, underscore the importance of the employee's work, add interest and challenge to the job, increase the employee's responsibility and autonomy, serve toward continuous learning and personal improvement, and place emphasis on other personal achievements rather than depending exclusively on money rewards.

Name of teacher or classified employee:

_____

Present Assignment:_____

Date: _____

Please give your attention to the following personal interest questionnaire. Its purpose is to gain your feedback regarding your work experiences thus far this school year. In some questions we ask about your current work assignment and the extent to which you are finding satisfaction on the job. We especially are interested in your personal recommendations for making the work responsibilities more enjoyable for you. What might be done to support your efforts? What program assignments might be changed? Are your present extra-curriculum assignments meeting your expectations? Although it might not be possible to change your teaching assignments or work activities for next semester, please know that your interests will be given serious consideration.

Thomas Scott, Principal

1. If possible, what changes would you like to see in your teaching or job assignments next semester or in the immediate future?

   _____

2. What changes, if any, would you recommend in your extra-curricular assignments?

   _____
   _____
   _____
   _____
   _____

3. What instructional support might be helpful to you (e.g., instructional supplies, teaching intern, preparations, work environment, communication processes, maintenance supplies, workload, work schedule, etc.)?

   _____
   _____
   _____
   _____
   _____
   _____

Figure 3.1. An Example Personal Interest Questionnaire

4. Which school or school system or work committee is of most interest to you? Our school committees include the curriculum committee, the personnel committee, the parent relations committee, the negotiations committee, the student activities committee, the student council, program evaluation committee and health & safety committee.

_____
_____
_____
_____
_____

5. To what extent have your interests and needs for continuous improvement been met? What recommendations might you have in this regard?

_____
_____
_____
_____
_____

6. What factors loom important in keeping you with us in the Wymore School District? Are there matters that need our attention/improvement in this regard? Please give us your feedback in terms of suggestions and recommendations.

_____
_____
_____
_____
_____
_____

Figure 3.1.   Continued

An identified best practice in employee retention is that of offering *retention-focused* benefits. Retention bonuses, helping employees to achieve excellence in their work responsibilities, and making a special effort to help the employee implement best practices that are successful methods for achieving the desired results of the job at hand are examples of retention-focused benefits. Retention-focused benefits are provisions that are implemented to receive the best return on human and material resources investments (return on investment).

THE RECRUITMENT PROCESS: WITHOUT WHICH NOT!

There is no shortage of licensed teachers nationally. It is just that thousands of persons with appropriate licenses do not enter the teaching profession. There are other problems that militate against the maintenance of a sufficient pool of candidates for teaching positions, such as non-competitive compensation and disparate salaries among the states and school districts within a state.

The levels of adequate preparation for teaching vary widely, and reports indicate that most of the neediest school districts are paying less for teaching personnel. Varying work conditions, inequitable load assignments, lack of needed school equipment and supplies, unhealthy school climates, and lack of effective mentoring support are among other factors that detract from the attractiveness of teaching as a lifelong profession.

Effective recruitment programs are founded on effective planning and forecasting strategies. The HR office historically has established the recruitment needs and purposes, advertised position openings, held applicant interviews with potential candidates, and selected the most qualified applicants for interviews by the appropriate local school principals and/or selection teams. Today, these procedures remain in place but the local school principal and school recruitment teams have become more prominent. We often hear the statement that every teacher and classified employee is a recruiter of school personnel. This contention that every teacher is a teacher recruiter has grown in importance due to the increasing competition for talented people.

PERSONNEL RECRUITMENT STRATEGIES

Tips for enhancing personnel recruitment are many and are not particularly new or consistent recommendations. One widely practiced activity is the job fair that is carried out in varying ways and at different sites. The advice of advertising widely is voiced frequently along with the advice to focus on recruiting local talent. We are told to highlight salaries unless they might not be competitive and in that case told to highlight teacher support, mentoring services, professional development opportunities, and other affective characteristics to sell the school district.

It is a good idea to partner with universities and colleges for identifying potential teacher prospects, but you need to avoid those institutions that have questionable records of quality preparation programs. Give hiring bonuses or bonuses for first-year employees who remain for a second year in the school system if the money is available. You might entice a potential candidate by reducing the workload for first-year teachers or by giving them the first chance to have a student teacher in their classroom.

Recruitment has become increasingly competitive. Recruiting and hiring practices all too often have kept potential hires in the dark. The war for talent is requiring human resources directors to develop new skills and initiate innovative strategies for the recruitment process. The HR unit of the school district must implement tracking systems in the recruitment process that keep the unit in close contact with potential job candidates. Effective communication relative to the specific district processes for recruitment and hiring is viewed as a best practice: this is who we are, what we do, how we can help you achieve your goals, and why you should join our educational team.

We asked several HR directors what they did purposely to attract and retain teachers. The most common response from the directors was the practice of including veteran teachers in the recruiting process. When conducting interviews at a university or college site, several directors included a teacher who had graduated from the institution being visited. Another popular response was that of stressing the availability of a positive school climate and staff support that works for teachers. Such support included purposeful mentoring that is planned and implemented as opposed to just giving new teachers a cooperative teacher who is available to answer questions concerning school procedures.

Those human resources directors serving in districts with competitive salaries emphasized this fact in their visits with teacher prospects. Although bonuses were mentioned by only a few of the HR directors, they recommended this provision as being especially attractive. Most new personnel entering the teaching field are facing some debt and current costs of moving, housing, and transportation. Approximately one-fourth of the directors reported that teachers received stipends for defraying costs of teaching supplies.

The practice of arranging collaborative planning time was reported as a point of interest to teachers entering the profession, as was the factor of cooperative teacher-administrator relationships. One human resources director noted that her school system recently implemented performance-based pay that the school leaders were hoping would be a positive influence on the retention of new personnel. Another director reported that his school system had given much attention to assessing and improving the climate within all schools in the district. The positive results of this activity were emphasized in interviews with prospective position candidates.

IDENTIFYING RECRUITMENT SOURCES: A PROACTIVE PROCESS

The teachers and classified employees should be informed that employee recruitment is the business of everyone. Classified personnel within the school system commonly have knowledge of other individuals that might be interested in changing jobs or taking advantage of the work benefits offered by the school district. One successful recruitment strategy is to guarantee an interview to every new applicant. Keep a close contact and positive relationship with teacher placement offices at local colleges and universities. Work with the local teacher preparation programs to gain the services of students that must do student teaching and make special efforts to orient them to the school district and the advantages of working in the school system.

Most every school program offers programs in the areas of business, industrial arts, agriculture, the social sciences, safety and health services, family living, and other related careers. Why not a course or program related to education? A relationship with a Future Teachers of America program should be implemented in every school district's curricular program. In social studies and civics courses, a unit on education and its importance for supporting a democratic nation seems appropriate. How does one become a teacher and what are the actual benefits and opportunities of a career as a professional educator? In every school situation, there are highly qualified staff to serve as instructors in a school program on education.

Local school community organizations are likely to have resources for providing student scholarships for fostering student interests in social work and other community enterprises. Use the available media such as the local newspapers, radio, television, and community theaters to promote the school and advertise its position opportunities. Be certain that all media and recruitment brochures are professionally designed and illustrated.

School districts have numerous internal and external recruitment sources. In fact, internal employees have been shown to be excellent sources for identifying potential certified and classified employees. The human resources director will enhance the recruitment process by supporting the theme, "Every school district employee is an employee recruiter." One strategy is that of training in-district recruiters. Such trainees can serve as *scouts* at various community/state events with a view to persuading or stimulating the interest of an individual to apply for positions in the school district.

In-house recruiters can serve to extend recruiting efforts throughout the network. Keeping employees informed of the school district's forecasts of employee needs will prove beneficial. Social media skills are a must for HR directors. Most everyone has experienced being given a discount on services by a dentist, auto mechanic, or other business by recommending a new client who does business with that concern. In view of the high costs of personnel recruitment, what about giving some monetary reward to school staff personnel that recommend employees for the school district that ultimately are hired?

Other internal recruiting sources include walk-ins, prior applications on record, and networking with school principals and other school employees within the school district. External sources include a wide variety of potential recruitment sources: newspaper advertising, ads on the Web, retired persons, employment agencies, training organizations, career development offices within the state, recruitment agencies, job search firms, job banks, and job fairs are among those sources. Blogging on social network sites might work for you. Successful recruitment results are contingent on proactive strategies.

POTENTIAL HIRES WELCOME DEVELOPMENT OPPORTUNITIES

Classified employee effectiveness is closely tied to opportunities for personal development. Such activities serve to enhance career development, improve job production, and provide opportunities for career advancement. It is common for classified employees to earn training credits that lead to salary scale advancements as well as higher positions within the job family. For example, a typist clerk could participate in special training that ultimately leads to higher positions as a staff secretary or secretary of administrative services. An account clerk 1, with required training, could improve his or her position to become an accounting technician, budget control clerk, payroll clerk, or senior account clerk.

Each of the foregoing suggestions can add positively to the school district's recruitment pool. Talent competition today requires appropriate and immediate responses to employment inquiries. Some school districts have approved the "hiring" of an obviously highly qualified candidate "on the spot." That is, the red tape that sometimes is required by the recruitment and selection processes leads to loss of talented candidates. Using the on-the-spot hiring strategy, of course, is contingent on obtaining the agreement of the school superintendent and the final approval by the school board; such actions commonly are expedited.

THE PRIMARY IMPORTANCE OF
THE POSITION DESCRIPTION

The effectiveness of the recruitment process can be enhanced if a specific position description has been completed and then utilized in determining applicants who are perceived as being best fits for candidacy. A position description gives the position applicant a written view of the nature of the position in question and also provides the search committee a resource for developing relevant interview questions. Below is an example of the major contents commonly included in a position description for a classroom teacher.

A position description for a classified employee would be similar but might give more attention to such factors as working conditions, physical effort required in the position, safety measure requirements, and varying work schedules that many classified work positions demand.

The Content Areas for Classroom Teacher's Position Description

Position Title
Position Qualifications: Licensure, Degrees, Experience, etc.
Supervision Received
Supervision Given
Primary Position Goals/Objectives: Learning Standards
Position Responsibilities: Preparation, Lesson Planning, Classroom Climate, Curriculum Standards, Relations, Record Keeping, Implementation of Policies/Procedures, Professional Development and Other Activities Expected of the Classroom Teacher
Special Skills and Knowledge: Cognitive and Affective Characteristics Related to Effective Student Performance
Terms of Employment: Salary, Benefits, Classroom Assignments, Special Duties, Extra-Curricular Assignments, etc.
Performance Evaluation: School Board Policy on Performance Evaluations and Assessments, State Law Requirements

Other Important Position Requirements as Required by the Local School(S), School Board, State, and Federal Agencies.

ORGANIZING FOR RECRUITMENT

Recruitment organization centers on providing guidelines for implementing the recruitment process, including work responsibilities, financial support, employee needs data, position analyses and descriptions, qualified interviewers, report forms, and related communication activities. The establishment of the applicant pool(s) includes giving additional attention to criteria for the purpose of defining the applicant pool and later the selection of the highest qualified personnel to become candidates for the positions in question.

Controlling the recruitment process includes a continuous monitoring of its implementation and the follow-up evaluation and assessment of its effectiveness. To what extent were the purposes of the recruitment process accomplished? What procedures proved to the most successful and why? What procedures did not produce the desired outcomes? What changes in the recruitment process need to be improved, and what support/leadership is needed to implement these changes? Answers to these questions and others center on actions of accountability of the human resources director's office.

One example of controlling the recruitment process and checking the HR unit's accountability is that of assessing yield ratios. The strategy centers on determining the success of recruitment and selection ratios. Consider the situation whereby fifty pool applicants ultimately were selected as candidates for forty-seven position openings; the recruitment rating would be 106%. On the other hand, if only thirty-seven applicants were selected for candidacy for the forty-seven positions, the rating would be 79%.

THE BENEFITS OF METRICS HAVE BECOME EVIDENT

Consider a situation of a school system that has 200 original position applications. Of this number, 150 were placed in the recruitment applicant pool. The yield ratio would be 75%. Of the 150 persons in the applicant pool, 100 were selected for position candidates, giving a yield ratio of 66.7%. Of the 100 position candidates, 50 became position finalists, resulting in a yield ratio of 50%. Of the 50 position finalists, 45 were offered contracts, for a yield ratio of 90%. All of the 45 candidates accepted contracts, for an acceptance ratio of 100%. And, lastly, 35 of the 45 new teachers accepted contracts and remained after the first year of teaching, for a yield ratio of 77.7%. Of this group of teachers, 25 remained in the school system after year 3 for a retention yield ratio of 71.4% (Breaugh, 1997).

Such data serve several beneficial purposes. For example, it might be important for the personnel director to know the reasons that 50 of the original 200 applicants were not retained in the applicant pool. Also, the school system lost almost 25% of its first-year teachers. One important goal would be to set an objective to reduce this loss figure. At which times in the recruitment process was the retention ratio most positive and why? Such assessment as the foregoing yield ratio strategy is an example of the kinds of self-evaluation that can be beneficial to the work of the HR director.

HUMAN RESOURCES METRICS FOR SHARPENING OPERATIONAL PRACTICES

The following section recommends several uses of metrics that can give the HR director important data relative to the effectiveness and efficiency of HR practices. In the foregoing sections of this chapter, we discussed metrics relative to the recruitment and hiring processes. Extended metrics for the recruitment and hiring processes can serve key information relative to costs per vacancy, costs per hire, search fees, and other metrics that can be used to assess the effectiveness and efficiencies of recruitment and hiring practices.

The following section provides a brief explanation of HR metrics that can provide valuable information for improved decision making. Some metrics are quite simple and straightforward, and others are a bit more complex. For example, we have recommended in this chapter that the school district's employees become recruiters for the school system. Now that this recommendation has been stated, to what extent is it being carried out? Simply track the actual applicants received for position openings and track the sources for their referral. Are the school district employees actually recommending school district job openings to others in the company?

Jacobson (2013) recommends using metrics to judge the *quality of hire* (QoH). This metric requires some tracking in that the average job performance rating of hires is required along with the percentage of new hires reaching acceptable productivity ratings and the percentage of hires that are retained after one year. Assume that the average job performance rating of the new classified hires after an acceptable time period was 75%; the percentage of the new hires reaching acceptable productivity ratings was 70%; and 80% of the new hires were retained after one year. (The average of 75% + 70% + 80% = QoH of 75%.) It would be up to the HR director, school principal, and other related supervisors to determine if the resulting metric was satisfactory or not. In addition, each one of the three statistics would be most likely considered if improvement programs in place had been effective.

Another important metric is that of talent retention. Donaldson (2013) suggests that it isn't enough to have a high retention rate if you are losing key talent. School districts commonly lose 20% to 30% of their certificated personnel after one year of service. Assume that the school district was losing 25% of its new hires after one year and 15% of them were viewed as high-quality teachers. Assume that the school was losing 25% of its new hires after one year and 60% were viewed as high quality teachers. If the school hired 50 new teachers, it loses 12.5 of the after the first year and approximately 8 of them are of high quality. We have discussed teacher retention in some depth previously in the chapter.

Certain metrics can be of great value in identifying and reducing flight risks in school settings. This is why such metrics as retention rates, retention rates within various schools, compensation metrics, job satisfaction metrics, culture and diversity metrics, engagement metrics, workforce age metrics, employee development metrics, and recognition metrics are not only important but essential for successful human resources programs today.

THE BENEFITS OF RECOGNITION ANALYTICS

Recognition analytics must be given serious attention as well. Jacobson (2013) points out that recognition analytics will let the HR director visualize cooperative relationships and effective communication among workgroups. Open communication channels and effective feedback loops in the school organization can be fostered by encouraging bonds of recognition among employees. The point is that you must ensure that you are facilitating communication and providing effective opportunities for employee involvement in activities and programs that affect their work and work environment.

School districts commonly report employee retention rates for the district as a whole. It might be insightful to examine retention rates by individual schools in the district. Although the resignation rate for the school district might be 20%, which individual schools are consistently retaining and/or losing voluntary personnel? Which levels of the school district are doing the best job of retaining qualified employees and which levels—elementary, middle, or high school—have the highest retention rates? With such metric information on hand, the HR director is much more prepared to determine the reasons for employee flight or stability and what steps must be taken to remedy or enhance the situations at hand.

THE IMPORTANCE OF JOB ANALYSIS
FOR CLASSIFIED PERSONNEL

The vital importance of job analysis was discussed earlier in the chapter. All of the reasons for having each job analyzed loom important for classified personnel as well. However, the importance of job analysis for classified positions is additionally significant for reasons of position grading and ulti-mate assessment of compensation levels. Each job within a job family is evaluated and assessed according to several criteria, including (1) skill and knowledge, (2) environment factors, (3) level of responsibility, (4) human relationship, (5) educational requirements, (6) level of experience, and (7) availability of talented personnel for the position in question. The following two criteria for 1 and 3 above show how classified jobs are evaluated and assessed for compensation purposes.

Skill and Knowledge	*Point Level*
The Employee:	
a. requires no specialized knowledge	1
b. requires a specialized skill/knowledge common to all broad categories	2
c. requires a specialized skill/knowledge not common to all in the category	3
d. requires a high level of skill/knowledge not common to all in the category	4
Level of Responsibility	
The Employee	
a. is responsible only for the satisfactory performance of his or her own work	1
b. is responsible for his or her own work but does some work independently	2
c. is responsible for the direction of an office and/or unit of employees	3
d. is responsible for the function of a subdivision of the system and helps develop policy which aids in making decisions that aid in goal achievement	4

Norton (2008, p. 376).

The total point level for each position is totaled and considered for job grading and salary ranges. Salary ranges commonly vary from range 8 to range 45. Hourly pay within each job range is determined, and increases are allocated according to years of experience. For example, the hourly pay for a worker at range 8 might begin at $12.53 per hour. For the second year, the worker would receive an hourly payment increase and perhaps move to $13.16 per hour on the salary schedule.

THE SELECTION PROCESS AS THE KEY TO PROGRAM EFFECTIVENESS

The selection of highly qualified personnel for assuming the educational responsibilities of the school system is viewed by the large majority of human resources directors as the most important responsibility that they do. Personnel selection for both professional and classified personnel commonly includes the planning, designing, and organizing of the selection process, clarifying the affective and cognitive characteristics to be considered for position selections, gathering appropriate selection data through application forms, interviewing, examining applicant/candidate records, obtaining references, testing strategies, arranging background checks, and evaluating/ assessing the selection results.

The *planning* and *organizing* of the selection process includes the attention given to the school district's selection policy, developing appropriate selection purposes/goals, discussing strategic plans and responsibilities of selection leaders, and reviewing the position descriptions for the job openings to be filled. The considerations of staff balance relative to such factors as experience, gender, race, and interests are among the topics discussed by the search/selection team.

Defining the affective and cognitive characteristics important for each position opening is significant for realizing an appropriate staff mix. Behavioral characteristics are gathered through various sources, including the position application, personal references, preliminary and final personal interviews, past work experiences, and personal observation. The interviewing process is given special attention from the outset of the applicant's application to the final position interview involving each finalist candidate.

HOW AN EFFECTIVE APPLICATION FORM BENEFITS THE HR PROCESSES OF RECRUITMENT AND SELECTION

An effectively developed application form provides information that can be used to help determine the applicant's placement in the recruitment pool. If an applicant's qualifications do not meet the requirements for the position in question, it is always best, as a professional courtesy, to relate this fact to the applicant at the earliest possible time. Although the information to be gathered from the application form does vary, it commonly includes the record of the individual's educational experience, educational degrees held and licensure certificates, required references, and other requested information such as official transcripts, test scores, GPAs, and related experience.

Applicants who are approved for the recruitment pool are informed that a background check also is required if the individual is hired. In summary, the major components of the application form includes the following: (1) personal data, (2) certifications held, (3) teaching experience, (4) preparation record (undergraduate and post-graduate credits), (5) position desired, (6) written responses to appropriate performance questions, and (7) names, position, addresses, and relationship of professional references (former work supervisors to be included).

In order to expedite the screening process, many school districts have implemented electronic screening. According to the specifications desired for a specific position, information in the database is used to locate and rank order the applicants to date. If certain applicants stand out among the group, a follow-up contact is completed commonly by telephone. These persons are viewed as position candidates, and a personal interview is scheduled at the earliest possible time. Also, the way that the applicant responds over the telephone might serve to "weed out" the applicant pool.

Other applicants remaining in the applicant pool are selected to participate in an initial screening interview for the purposes of (1) verifying the correctness of the application information, (2) expressing interest in the applicant's qualifications, (3) answering questions of clarification for the applicant, and (4) asking questions of the applicant that center on the special needs of the position or serve to assess the applicant's oral communication or to clarify an answer stated by the applicant on the application form.

The HR person involved in an initial screening interview with an applicant might ask the applicant a strategy question such as "You mentioned in your application form that student achievement was a high priority in your teaching. Just what do you do to engage students in the learning process?" Preliminary interviews are generally brief and positively structured. When effectively structured, an applicant screening interview could last no more than five minutes. This being the case, an interviewer most likely could complete twelve such interviews in about one hour.

Depending on the case at hand, an employment interview might be scheduled at the time of the screening interview. Why "rush" the process? After all, making a bad hire commonly has long-lasting and troublesome consequences. Yes, but a great hire can be long lasting and problem-less. How can one identify a great teacher even before hiring one and seeing him or her teach for several months? Great teachers have been identified by their affective characteristics, such as caring/loving, effective communication skills, enthusiasm, a sense of humor, fairness, and good listening skills, and, if they have had prior teaching experience, they foster a positive classroom climate.

In addition, great teachers have several important cognitive skills, including high test scores, high student expectations/standards/goals, high-quality preparation credentials, effective organizational abilities, effective teaching strategies, and student motivation skills, and are able to monitor student learning and meet student interests and needs (Norton, 2015).

Regardless of the kind of interview, a guiding purpose is to identify top performers. In the candidate stages of the interviewing process, questions can help the interviewer(s) to put an approval stamp on the candidate. It is important that the candidate has taken the advantage of learning about the school district and the nature of the position in question.

What improvements can we make with our educational program services to be more effective? Why are you interested in this specific position and what knowledge and skills do you believe you would bring to this position? What responsibilities in your past work experiences or present work have been most satisfying for you? Do you have any question? This last question serves to identify the candidate's interest in the position and to elaborate on his or her characteristics for contributing to the school and school district's educational program.

QUALITY INTERVIEWS REQUIRE QUALIFIED INTERVIEWERS

Effective practices for candidate interviews require the people doing the interviewing to be qualified to do so. Becoming a human resources director or school principal does not automatically give the person the knowledge and skills required for meaningful interviewing. Without such knowledge and skills, the interviewing results most often will be based on subjective opinions relative to the candidate's appearance, opinion statements, or other behaviors not directly related to the characteristics to be appraised. "The lack of interview training and dependency on the use of a 'sixth sense' for determining the best candidate are among the reasons for poor selection results" (Norton, 2008, p. 138).

Persons who participate in the selection process as interviewers must be able to demonstrate their knowledge and skills in several ways: (1) knowing and understanding the basic requirements of recruitment and selection as established by school board policy, (2) having a thorough knowledge of the position opening(s) for which the interview is being conducted, (3) being fully acquainted with the position and the basic affective and cognitive characteristics important for the teacher's or employee's role, (4) being able to understand and utilize the interview instrument, especially prepared to assess the behavior characteristics for the position opening in question, and (5) having the ability to maintain evaluation and assessment objectivity based on the special position requirements at hand. Focus on experience, talents, and qualifications in the decision of hire.

The selection of qualified interviewers includes the matters of (1) having time to perform the many requirements of interviewing and related criteria assessments, (2) having the qualifications required of objective interviewing, (3) having the sensitivity in human relations, poise, and temperament to serve as a candidate interviewer, and (4) having a performance record concerning employee interviewing results. Does the interviewer's record of selection recommendations show favorably with those of other qualified interviewers?

INTERVIEWING TECHNIQUES THAT PRODUCE RESULTS

The primary purpose of the selection interview is to focus on the selection criteria for the specific position opening in relation to the qualifications of the interviewee for meeting the expressed criteria. An underlying purpose is to enhance the candidate's interest in accepting a contract if indeed this option is desired. For example, assume that a female candidate's application form or screening interview revealed a special interest in dance. The question might be asked, "Might you be interested in organizing a dance club as your extra-curricular activity?" A prospective math teacher might be asked, "We have talked about having a math fair at the school where students, parents, and others could visit it at the school. Might that be something that you might like to help organize sometime in the future?"

Short interviews, long interviews, and group interviews are among the interview techniques recommended by Talent Attraction and Selection Systems. We suggest that the length of a candidate's selection interview depends primarily on one factor, and that is purpose. At this point in time, the interviewer should know a great deal about a position candidate's personal background and qualification. There is no need to spend more time on these topics.

Assume the prospect is a candidate for a teaching position in the primary grades. Grades 1 and 2 focus directly on introductory reading and word pronunciation. The interviewer might pose just one question in the short interview, "How do you teach word recognition?" The interviewer's response regarding the importance of phonics and related word recognition strategies such as semantic or meaning clues, syntactic or word clues, picture clues, or context clues might serve the purpose of determining if the individual should be invited to participate in an on-site performance interview.

Candidates who are invited for an on-site interview might be asked to participate in a *performance interview*. A performance interview provides an opportunity to observe the candidate's performance relative to knowledge of the subject at hand, confidence and poise, oral communication, and instructional methods. In one actual case, the math teacher candidate was asked to demonstrate the teaching of the number system. The candidate went to the chalkboard, picked up a piece of chalk, and quite quickly spoke of the common base 10 decimal number system.

She then noted that there are many other number systems that are used today; one is the binary system that has only two digits, 0 and 1. "OK," said the candidate, "Let's all count together using the binary number system." Together, the interviewers started by saying "one, two . . ." "Hold on now," said the candidate. "Where did you find that number 2?" she said, "We only have a number 0 and a number 1 in our new system. So we write 1, 2, 3, 4,

5 in the binary system as 1, 10, 11, 100, 101, and so on. We read this binary number as one, twin, twin one, twindred, twindred one, and so on."

The place values for the decimal system are as follows: 100,000 (from right to left): 10^0, 10^1, 10^2, 10^3, 10^4, 10^5). "Similarly, in the binary system, the number 100,000 (from right to left): 2^0, 2^1, 2^2, 2^3, 2^4, 2^5, which is equal to $0 + 2 + 4 + 8 + 16 + 32$ in the decimal number system." As one might expect, the interview group was impressed. The interviewee had the interviewers engaged in the lesson.

The *long interview technique* uses various strategies and activities to assess the candidate's strengths and weaknesses. The candidate might spend an entire morning or afternoon at the school site touring the school facilities and meeting with school personnel, students, and parents. A consensus assessment is determined for the candidates on the basis of the selection criteria selected prior to the interview. The candidate has ample opportunity to see the school and facilities in which he or she would be teaching. During the long interview, the candidate would have the opportunity to meet most every member of the staff and to speak to the teaching staff related to his or her subject area.

Subject-specialty interviews are designed to gather information especially related to the position opening. In these cases, the interview form centers on the content areas of preparation, knowledge, and skills related to the subject at hand; specific preparation and experience; personal characteristics considered most important for the position opening (communication skills, enthusiasm, sensitivity, relationships); and other behavior characteristics. For example, the screening dimension for an English teacher candidate commonly would include a check on degrees and majors in the field, GPAs in English studies, knowledge of English curriculum, special interest/knowledge in various areas of English, such as composition, literature, speech, drama, grammar, reading, and communication skills.

The *structured interview* evolved as a popular interviewing strategy in the early 1960s. The strategy uses a series of prepared questions accompanied by specific *look-fors* to assess characteristics such as mission, empathy, individualized perception, listening, focus, and innovation. The teacher perceiver instrument initially was researched and designed by Donald Clifton and William Hall, both professors at the University of Nebraska-Lincoln at the time. Each of the characteristics assessed by the teacher perceiver instrument is one not readily determined by other interview strategies. For example, how does an interviewer learn of a candidate's characteristic of empathy?

The *teacher perceiver* determined the extent of this quality by asking certain questions over and over with the candidate's answers profiled and charted. That is, a question related to the characteristic of empathy would be set forth in a scenario for the candidate's reflection. "Assume that you found a sophomore student crying by his locker in the school hallway. You approach the student and ask, 'What seems to be the problem?' The student replies that his best friend, Jerry, was picked up by the police for shoplifting and he had been suspended from school. What would you do in this situation?" The interviewer awaits the candidate's response.

The characteristic of empathy would be shown if the candidate refrained from lecturing the boy about the penalties of such illegal behavior or lecturing him about the fact that the behaviors of his friend should serve as a lesson for him. Rather, the empathetic teacher would praise the student for a caring attitude toward the problems of his friend. If the teacher indicated that he or she would follow up on the matter to see how the friend might be helped, the teacher would receive additional credit.

WISE USE OF TESTING

The use of such methods as candidate testing tends to increase or decrease with the variations in the availability of employee candidates. In other situations, the trustworthiness of a potential employee might be highly important. The *Workplace Productivity Profile* is a personality assessment that is used to help predict whether an individual will be conscientious, productive, and reliable. The test measures four traits: conscientiousness, perseverance, integrity/honesty, and attitudes toward theft and fraud. It is used widely as a selection instrument for positions such as security guards, persons who handle cash, service technicians, production workers, cashiers, secretaries, and other positions where attendance, punctuality, work ethic, and trustworthiness are valued.

General intelligence tests have revealed a 0.51 predictability of future job success for jobs with average demands. When coupled with an integrity test, the predictability increases to 0.65. Assessment center techniques became popular in the 1980s for selecting administrative personnel. Assessment center participants worked through tasks designed to demonstrate behaviors of effective administrators. Assessment center methods alone revealed a low 0.37 performance statistic for future job success. When coupled with a general intelligence test statistic of 0.51, the success statistic was 0.53, an increase of only 0.02 (Schmidt & Hunter, 1998).

WHY EVALUATE AND ASSESS SELECTION RESULTS?

Unless a planned and purposeful evaluation of selection results becomes an ongoing activity, the process of selection has little chance of improvement.

Just as with the case of any personnel activity, the selection process carries with it the major consideration of accountability. What primary purposes for selection were established at the outset and to what extent were these purposes accomplished?

Which selection activities proved most effective and why? Were interviewers adequately trained to participate effectively in the selection process? What collected data were especially useful in the selection process? What selection activities need to receive priority attention? How will the overall success of this year's selection process be identified and assessed?

A school board report is fair evidence of accountability. A thorough selection report shows the extent to which the human resources selection procedures complement the school board's recruitment and selection policy. The report can indicate the results of the school board's support of the personnel function generally and personnel selection specifically. The report can underscore the problems being encountered in certain HR processes and the need to give attention to additional support for personnel selection if indeed this is a definite concern.

POST-QUIZ

Take a few minutes to complete the final quiz on teacher placement and orientation activities. Mark true or false for each statement posed but avoid just guessing the answer. Check your score at the end of the quiz.

1. A teacher signs a teaching contract that specifies that he will teach five classes of social studies each day. Nevertheless, the school principal can assign him to one class of physical education along with four classes of social studies regardless of the teacher's objections. ____True or ____ False

2. If an elementary school teacher signed a contract that indicated that she was hired as a third-grade teacher, she could not be assigned to teach another grade unless she agreed to do so. ____ True or ____ False

3. A contract assignment to teach in the school district does give the school district the authority to place the teacher in any school within the district that has the grade(s) or subject(s) that the contract sets forth. ____ True or ____ False

4. A teacher's beliefs are contrary to such controversial subjects as abortion rights, gay rights, and same-sex marriages. However, the teacher signed a contract to teach in the curriculum area in which these subjects have been approved by the state and school board. Nevertheless, the teacher can refuse to teach these subjects. ____ True or ____ False

5. Research has supported the concept of tailoring the teaching position to suit the person. ____ True or ____ False

6. The HR orientation process is the one- or two-day in-service program (just before school starts in the fall) that gives new teachers information about school resources and student discipline measures and also answers questions that most every new teacher wants to ask. ____ True or ____ False

7. One educational researcher found that personal assistance given to teachers new to the school system was the single most important factor for fostering teacher morale ____ True or ____ False

8. The workload of new teachers is often found to be the heaviest among all the teaching staff. ____ True or ____ False

9. Although teacher workload is commonly unfairly distributed among a school's staff, the school system has yet to find a way to measure teacher workload and examine equity assignments. ____ True or ____ False

10. Studies of orientation activities for new teachers commonly rate "additional time provided to prepare" high on the list of most effective. ____ True or ____ False

Answers to the Post-Quiz

Question 1 is false; question 2 is true; question 3 is true; question 4 is false; question 5 is false; question 6 is false; question 7 is true; question 8 is true; question 9 is false; question 10 is true.

Scoring Results

Your Score

10–9 Correct—You receive five stars *****: Apply for the position of HR director.

8–7 Correct—You receive four stars ****: Take charge of your school's placement/orientation activities.

6–5 Correct—You receive three stars ***: Request a leadership role in the next orientation program.

4–3 Correct—You receive two stars **: Reread this chapter with special attention to orientation.

2–1 Correct—You receive one star *: Review the section on placement/orientation—retake test.

0 Correct—Sorry, you are out of stars: Review the answers for the quiz, and then give your attention to chapter 4.

Discussion of the Post-Quiz

1. Question 1, "A teacher signs a teaching contract that specifies that he will teach five classes of social studies each day. Nevertheless, the school principal can assign him to one class of physical education along with four classes of social studies regardless of the teacher's objections," is false. Courts have ruled that a signed contract determines the nature of the teacher's assignment and cannot be unilaterally changed unless the teacher agrees to the change. Any changes in the contract must be agreed upon by both parties.

2. Question 2, "If an elementary school teacher signed a contract that indicated that she was hired as a third-grade teacher, she could not be assigned to teach another grade unless she agreed to do so," is true. Although the contract's specifications determine the teacher's assignment, in some cases the assignment is less specific. For example, the contract might specify that the teacher is assigned to the primary grades or to teach at the elementary school level. Of course, this leaves the placement assignment open to several grade options.

3. Question 3, "A contract assignment to teach in the school district does give the school district the authority to place the teacher in any school within the district that has the grade(s) or subject(s) that the contract sets forth," is true. However, if the teacher contract states that the teacher is to teach grade 3, the school district cannot assign the teacher to another grade level unless the teacher agrees to do so.

4. Question 4, "A teacher's beliefs are contrary to such controversial subjects as abortion rights, gay rights, and same-sex marriages. However, the teacher signed a contract to teach in the curriculum area in which these subjects have been approved by the state and school board. Nevertheless, the teacher can refuse to teach these subjects," is false. The state board of education in most states and the local school board are the legal authorities as to what is taught in the curriculum. Refusal to teach the subjects agreed to in the contract would be a violation of the contract and also considered a matter of insubordination.

5. Question 5, "Research has supported the concept of tailoring the teaching position to suit the person," is false. On the contrary, it is clear that selection of personnel is to focus fitting the person to the position at hand. This perspective underscores the importance of developing a factual position description for every job and using it to collect relevant information for the recruitment and selection of personnel. The implementation of job analysis also looms important in this respect.

6. Question 6, "The HR orientation process is the one- or two-day in-service program (just before school starts in the fall) that gives new teachers

information about school resources and student discipline measures and also answers questions that most every new teacher wants to ask," is false. Orientation is a comprehensive ongoing process that begins with the initial recruitment activities whereby the mission of the school system and its professional opportunities are advertised and the nature of the school system and its employees is addressed. Although certain activities are focused on helping the new employees get a successful start in the position he or she has assumed, orientation relative to policies, programs, practices, needs, purposes, and improvements are carried out throughout the entire school year. Orientation ultimately works its way into individual development plans for each employee who comes under the HR process of staff development.

7. Question 7, "One educational researcher found that personal assistance given to teachers new to the school system was the single most important factor for fostering teacher morale," is true (Berglas, 1973). Another study by Lemke (1995) revealed a significant contribution of orientation as related to teacher retention. Lemke's study found that an effectively planned and implemented induction program resulted in increasing teacher retention rates by 50% to 85%. We submit that studies such as the foregoing research should be replicated and if the results remain valid the information should be widely disseminated.

8. Question 8, "The workload of new teachers is often found to be the heaviest among all the teaching staff," is true. In an early teacher load study by Norton (1959), the average teaching load, average cooperative load, and average teaching load were calculated for 335 secondary school teachers. The Douglass Teacher Load Formula was used to calculate the total teaching load index for each teacher participant.

The cooperative load of the teacher includes those work responsibilities outside the classroom, such as committee work, in-service development, and other extra-curricular assignments. The teaching load plus the cooperative load is added to give the total teacher load index. In Norton's study, teachers with no experience (first-year teachers) had the highest teacher load index. Teachers with thirty or more years of experience had the lowest teacher load index. When the cooperative load was added to the teaching load, however, teachers with one to four years of experience were carrying the highest teacher load by a very small margin. First-year teachers ranked second in relation to the teacher load statistic.

We point out that the purpose of determining teacher load is not to find out who is working the hardest. Rather, the purpose is to determine inequities in load assignments and adjust loads to meet personnel and program purposes. Teacher load studies have found that some teachers in the same school have load indices two to three times greater than others with the lightest loads.

9. Question 9, "Although teacher workload is commonly unfairly distributed among a school's staff, the school system has yet to find a way to measure teacher workload and examine equity assignments," is false. Answer to question 8 should make it clear that education has had the means for measuring teacher load for many years. The Douglass Teacher Load Formula developed in 1950 (Douglass, 1951) has been used in numerous teacher load studies nationally. In addition, Norton and Bria developed a teacher load formula for measuring the load of elementary school teachers as early as 1992.

10. Question 10, "Studies of orientation activities for new teachers commonly rate 'additional time provided to prepare' high on the list of most effective," is true. One cannot help think about just how much attention is given to evaluating the orientation activities relative to their benefits for meeting teachers' interests and needs.

Purposes of the orientation process loom important. It seems quite clear that orientation topics for teachers new to the school need to be given priority attention. Common concerns that are encountered by those teachers new to the school and school system need to be given special attention: (1) instructional resources (human and material) that are available to them; (2) how to handle the grading system used in the school; (3) daily reports that are required, such as student absences and tardies; (4) student discipline guidelines; (5) student homework requirements; (6) parental involvement; (7) extra-curricular responsibilities; (8) sources of teacher support in relation to curriculum matters; (9) sources of special help concerning childcare, family care, health services, financial aid, and other support services.

A WORD ABOUT *TEACHER DISMISSAL*

It is not the purpose of this chapter to set forth an in-depth discussion of the many legal considerations affecting the administration of the personnel function. We refer the reader to the publication of Rowman & Littlefield's book *The Legal World of the School Principal: What Leaders Need to Know About School Law* (2016). Although the book does emphasize the work of the school principal and the surrounding legal implications of his or her decision-making responsibilities, all other certificated personnel and classified personnel in the school district will benefit by reading this resource.

The courts have made it clear that a teacher may not be removed for any other cause when the statutes specifically enumerate the causes for which a teacher may be discharged (*City of Elwood v. State*, 180 N.E. 4171, Ind. 1932). Even the use of the phrase *good or just cause* has its restrictions. Among the many reasons for teacher dismissal are health conditions, age, causing or supporting disruption, engaging in illegal activities, insubordination, incompetency or inefficiency, neglect of duty, unprofessional conduct, subversive activities, decreased need for services, marriage, civil rights activities, political activities, and reasons such as intoxication and use of drugs (Peterson et al., 1978).

Dismissal because of age does need some clarification. Peterson et al. (1978) point out that it has been well established that the state or boards of education can establish a retirement age. A mandatory retirement age that does not apply to other workers in the state may be established for teachers at the elementary and secondary school levels; such a regulation does not violate the Fourteenth Amendment.

THE EXIT INTERVIEW: WHO IS SAYING GOOD-BYE AND WHY?

Every organization inevitably will lose personnel. It is of special importance to learn why persons are voluntarily leaving the school system. An *exit interview* should be administered for several reasons of importance to the human resources function. An exit interview can be a valuable method of identifying the credibility of current personnel practices, and, in some cases, suggest changes that can be implemented to retain quality personnel. The following kinds of information can be secured through a face-to-face situation or in written form. The following questions are focused primarily on certificated personnel but with minor changes could be utilized for classified personnel as well who voluntarily plan to leave the school system.

One study asked voluntary separating personnel what they would like to change in the agency that they were leaving. Compensation and benefits was number one, with 1,674 responses. However, 1,482 persons named management/employee relations, 1,202 listed leadership, 1,164 checked employee rewards/recognition, 1,034 named internal policies and procedures, 1,015 checked work environment, 867 listed training, 678 listed resources, and 367 checked other reasons. It would appear that seven of the eight changes were changes that could not only be addressed but had reasonable possibilities of being changed in a more positive manner.

HR directors do not have magic wands to make such workplace changes. Nevertheless, management/employee relations, work environment, training, policies and procedures, and other needed changes have great potential for positive improvement with sincere and effective HR leadership knowledge and skills. A primary need on the part of HR directors is to give serious attention to building a culture of participation within the school system and the school community.

Just having a unifying mission can serve to build trust within the system. We submit that skill in building cooperative relationships within your school system will increase trust and will result in positive employee retention. As many authorities have stated, trust is more a matter of character than a matter of technique. Employees must be able to rely upon school leaders and experience positive teamwork and believable communication.

Exit Interview Sample Questions

1. What aspects of the position which you served did you like the best? What did you dislike about the position(s) you served?
2. Are you able to share with us your reasons for leaving the school/school system?
3. How would you describe the supervisory support that you received during your time in the school system?
4. How would you describe the climate in the school that you served? On the scale of 1 (low) to 10 (high), how would you rate the climate of the school(s) in which your served?
5. What can you tell us about the quantity and quality of the professional development activities provided for you?
6. What aspects of mentoring or coaching were available to you, and how would you rate their benefits to you personally?
7. To what extent did the school supervisors (principal, department head, grade-level leader) take advantage of your personal interests and strengths in your position assignment?
8. How were your career interests attended to in regard to coaching services, advancement, and professional growth during your services with the school system?
9. What two or three things might have been done by the school principal and other supervisors to be more helpful in meeting your position responsibilities?
10. How would you rate the human relationships in the school between teachers and students, teachers and the school administrators, and teachers and the school's parents?
11. What, if anything, might the school have done to retain your services? To what extent did compensation play a part in your decision to resign?
12. What other suggestions might you share with us regarding the school, school system, or teaching role in which you served?
13. Are you able to share with us your immediate or long-range plans?
14. This question would go to a person resigning to move to a new position in education: What were the major factors that attracted you to the position?

15. If the person expresses the fact that he or she just wants to take a break from teaching, the following question would be asked: Mighty you think about returning to teaching (or classified position) in the near future?

A MASTER'S DEGREE PROGRAM WITH A MAJOR IN HUMAN RESOURCES ADMINISTRATION

An Example of a Master's Degree with a Specialization in Human Resources Administration

The following degree program is not set forth as a model program that should be implemented in all school districts. Rather, it is one that establishes an emphasis on human resources administration with a sound foundation in administration/supervision, general education, research methods, and practicum in the field. The practicum experience might best be scheduled early in the student's course work. The internship could be split into 2 three-semester-hour experiences: one experience at the local school level and the second experience in the central office of the school district's human resources office.

EDA 501 Educational Administration & Supervision.	3 credit hours
EDA 502 The Human Resources Function and Certificated Personnel.	3 credit hours
EDA 503 The Human Resources Function and Classified Personnel	3 credit hours
EDA 504 School Policy and Administrative Regulation Development	3 credit hours
SED 501 Secondary Education Principles and Programs	3 credit hours
EED 501 Elementary Education Principles and Programs	3 credit hours
MED 501 Middle School Education Principles and Programs	3 credit hours
EDA 505 The Human Resources Director: Organizational Development	3 credit hours
EDA 506 Technical Components—Payroll, Benefits, Retirement	3 credit hours
PED 501 Research Methods/Project	3 credit hours
EDA 510 Practicum	3 credit hours
EDA 511 Human Resources Internship	3 credit hours

Key Chapter Ideas and Recommendations

• Changing forces on student enrollment in schools, including "competition" for students among public, private, and charter schools, financial support, and teacher retention, have resulted in increased attention to human resources processes such as re-recruitment, recruitment, orientation, and reduction in force.

- Calls for the improvement in the preparation of prospective education personnel is of high importance but must be supported by improvements in preparatory programs and supportive financial scholarships for prospective and practicing professional personnel. The positive results of having a specialty in human resources administration during the completion of the master's degree is highly recommended.
- The HR process of re-recruitment has been neglected in contemporary practice. New and innovative practices for retaining the services of highly qualified personnel must become a major priority of the HR function.
- Purposeful mentoring and high-quality orientation activities must be developed and implemented in every school district nationally. Just giving a new teacher a "cooperating teacher" is unsatisfactory. Successful orientation activities must the ongoing and initiated at the outset of an applicant's application for a position in the school system.
- School districts and local schools should initiate educational programs and activities for students that center on the importance of education and teaching in a democratic nation. Schools offer courses in a variety of careers, including business, industry, technology/science, social work, and health and welfare. Why not educate students relative to the importance of education relative to maintaining a democracy, supporting a free enterprise system, and giving each individual a fair chance to be successful in his or her life pursuits?
- The importance of completing position analyses and follow-up position descriptions must be re-instituted in schools in America. Outsourcing the development of school district policies and regulations and position descriptions militates against the concepts of involvement and commitment on the part of school district administrative leaders and school employees.
- Employee selection remains high on the list of most important processes of the HR function. Nevertheless, re-recruitment, placement, orientation, development, and other activities such as school climate loom important in the work of the human resources unit.
- The supporting activity of interviewing must be greatly improved. Quality interviewing centers on purposes, objectivity, and meaningful results. Just as special training in any important activity is essential, special preparation in interviewing must be required on the part of school personnel who are involved in interviewing activities. Quality interviewing leads to expeditious hiring.
- The placement of personnel in educational positions commonly is taken for granted; however, much of the costly turnover of classified and certificated personnel is due to a lack of important consideration of employee

placement. The human resources director must be fully aware of the laws relative employee placement. "Human resources authorities agree that one of the most effective means by which human resources administrators can assist the organization to achieve its stated goals and maximize employee potential is through the determination of appropriate position assignments" (Norton, 2008, p. 166).

DISCUSSION QUESTIONS

1. List several ways in which this chapter has widened your perspective on the role of the human resources director in education. For example, was the process of re-recruitment something that your school district has given importance?
2. Assume that you have been given the opportunity to address the parent-teacher organization in your school district. You'll have twenty-five minutes to address the topic Staffing the Wymore Public Schools. What key topics will you emphasize?
3. You have been asked to serve on a school district committee that will consider program innovations and recommendations for retaining quality personnel in both classified and professional teaching/administrative positions. Give some thought to how you personally would contribute to the thinking of the committee regarding the topic at hand.
4. Differentiate among an applicant interview, a behavioral interview, a long interview, and structured interview. How do these interviews differ and at what stage in the selection process might each interview strategy be appropriate?

CASE STUDIES

Case 3.1 Hiring of Classified Personnel Is Different; or Is It?

The human resources director of the Wymore School District was notified that both custodians at the Meadow Lark Middle School had resigned and their positions had to be filled by August 1, two weeks before the opening of school the next school year. George Nelson, principal of Meadow Lark Middle School, received a call from Phyllis Knowlton, director of classified personnel for the school district, and was told that she had six individuals in the classified candidates' pool that were available for custodial position interviews.

"George," asked director Nelson, "Could you select a school interview committee and let me know when you and committee members could schedule interviews with each of these candidates so I could make arrangements with each of them?"

"Do you mean that you want us to interview people for our custodial positions," responded Principal Nelson. "Since when did this procedure become necessary? Why don't you just pick out the two that you think are the best and hire them? I really do not know much about custodial work and I don't believe that members of my staff know much about that work either."

"As you know, George," stated Director Nelson, "the custodian is responsible to the school principal and the school principal is responsible for the supervision and evaluation of each classified employee in his or her school."

"It seems to me that something is missing here," said Principal Nelson. "I'd rather leave these hires strictly up to you."

Discussion Exercise

Take time to give serious thought to the scenario in case study 3.1. What does appear to be missing in this situation as presented? You might believe that communication is a problem, but if so what communication is missing here? As you review the case, give consideration to the work of the human resources director in relation to classified personnel but also give thought to the work of school principal and classified personnel. (Note that the classified staff are considered in chapter 5.)

REFERENCES

Berglas, W. W. (1973, November). A study of the relationships between induction practices and the morale of the beginning teacher. *Dissertation Abstracts International*, 34(5), 2189-A.

Breaugh, J. A. (1997). Yield ratios. In L. H. Peters, C. R. Green, & S. A. Youngblood (Eds.), *The Blackwell encyclopedia of human resources management* (pp. 257–258). Oxford, England: Blackwell.

Douglass, H. R. (1951). The 1950 revision of the high school teaching load formula. *NASSP Bulletin*, 35, 13–24.

Lemke, J. C. (1995). Attracting and retaining special education educators in rural and small schools: Issues and solutions. *Rural Special Education Quarterly*, 14(2), 25–30.

Mahoney, D. (2006). *Ethics and the school administrator.* Lanham, MD: Rowman & Littlefield Education.

Norton, M. S. (1959). *Teacher load in Nebraska high schools in cities from 5,000 to 25,000 population.* Lincoln, NE: University of Nebraska-Lincoln. An unpublished dissertation completed at the University under the supervision of Professor Leslie L. Chisholm.

Norton, M. S. (2008). *Human resources administration for educational leaders.* Thousand Oaks, CA: Sage.

Norton, M. S. (2009). *The personnel director in Arizona.: A research study.* Tempe, AZ: Arizona State University, Division of Leadership and Policy Studies, College of Education.

Norton, M. S. (2015). *Teachers with the magic: Great teachers change students' lives.* Lanham, MD: Rowman & Littlefield.

Norton, M. S. (2016). *What leaders need to know about school law.* Lanham, MD: Rowman & Littlefield.

Norton, M.S., & Bria, R. (1992). Toward an equitable measure of elementary school teacher load. *Record in Educational Administration and Supervision, 13*(1), 62–66.

Peterson, L.J., Rossmiller, R.A., & Volz, M.M. (1978). *The law and public school operation.* New York: Harper & Row.

Robinson, D.C., & Galpin, T. (1996, July). In for a change: Re-recruiting your "human capital" during turbulent times. *HR Magazine, 41*(7), 90–93.

Schmidt, F. L., & Hunter, E. (1998). The validity and utility of selection methods in personnel psychology: Practical and theoretical implication of 85 years of research findings. *Psychological Bulletin, 124,* 262–274.

Scott, D. (2012, August 23). *Biggest problem for public education? Lack of funding, poll says.* From the Web: http://www.governing.com/templates/gov_print_article?id=1670989185

Chapter 4

Toward the Maximization of Human Potential

> Primary chapter goal—To re-enforce the vital importance of the hiring process and to tie the HR processes of personnel orientation, development, and administrative management procedures to the maximization of the school system's human potential.

THE SELECTION PROCESS

> We shall never reach a time when it will not be necessary to erect new buildings in order to accommodate ourselves to the increase in population, but we have evidently passed the crisis in supplying the mechanical appliances necessary to a public school system, and now it is hoped that we have reached a period when a more liberal expenditure can be made in supplying that which alone can make an investment of twelve million dollars in school property really profitable, viz: the placing of a competent teacher in each school classroom. (Bloss, 1882, pp. 12, 13)

One hundred thirty-five years ago, Superintendent of Public Instruction John Bloss included the foregoing statement in his annual report to the State Board of Education of Indiana. This chapter gives emphasis to the hypothesis that his hope has yet to be fully accomplished.

We introduced the HR process of personnel selection in the previous chapter. That chapter emphasized the importance of recruiting and re-recruiting quality personnel. In this chapter, we delve more deeply into the selection process and tie it closely to the follow-up activities that foster positive continuous personnel growth and development.

Human resources directors commonly view the selection of personnel as the most important responsibility of the position. We ask you to respond to the following selection pre-quiz. By doing so, you will be able to "test" your current knowledge of the selection process in relation to both empirical and basic research. Select the correct/best response to each of the following fifteen selection questions and then check your answers with those provided at the end of the quiz. Avoid just guessing the answer; rather, skip that question move on to the next entry.

PRE-QUIZ

1. An effective selection process can serve the school and school district in many ways. It can
   a. serve to bring about needed changes in the school's and school district's programs and practices;
   b. bring new talent into the school program and thusly bring new thinking about the problems facing the school system;
   c. result in a bonding of the new employee and school leadership that fosters the potential of retaining talented personnel in the school system;
   d. upgrade the quality of program instruction and ultimately lead to improvements in student achievement;
   e. serve to improve the health of the school environment by improving the personnel relationships within the school and school district;
   f. improve all of the above.

2. An effective selection process is an indefinite endeavor since we have yet to find a way to determine the characteristics of great teachers and how to determine such characteristics in advance of hiring. ____True or ____False

3. A school board policy related to the hiring of personnel
   a. sets forth the administrative procedures for planning, designing, and implementing the selection process;
   b. simply includes the selection requirements set forth by state statutes;
   c. is a brief statement that delegates the personnel hiring responsibility to the district's school superintendent;
   d. sets forth the primary purposes/aims of the hiring process as opposed to the specific administrative procedures necessary for implementing the policy;
   e. includes all of the above;
   f. includes none of the above.

4. Which of the following is the best source for defining the behavioral characteristics to be used for rating of position candidates?
   a. A peer in a similar position
   b. The school principal in which the hired person will work

c. An effective position description for the job in question
d. A state department representative who is well acquainted with the subject or job family in question
e. None of the above
f. All of the above

5. Which characteristic ranked 1 of twenty-one characteristics named in one study by principals as being most important for teacher selection data?
   a. Pleasant personality
   b. Understanding of subject matter
   c. Effective discipline
   d. Respect for students
   e. Ability to be a decision maker
   f. None of the above

6. Which entry below best describes the purposes of an interview guide?
   a. It is the form sent to a position candidate that sets forth the format to be followed in the selection interview.
   b. It is the *scorecard* that lists the number ratings (1 [low] to 5 [high]) of the position candidate for each response given in the selection interview.
   c. It is a response letter completed by the position candidate prior to the interview.
   d. It gives directions/procedures for assessing the criteria relative to each position opening and provides guidelines for specific questions to be used in the interview.
   e. It is another name for a position description.
   f. None of the above.

7. TASS refers to "teacher affective, scholarship and socialization" characteristics. _____True or _____False

8. Which of the below entries is not a recognized interview technique used by school districts in the hiring process?
   a. Long interview technique
   b. Short interview technique
   c. Structured interview technique
   d. Performance interview technique
   e. Group interview technique
   f. Subject-specialty interview
   g. Telephone interview
   h. Waterboarding interview
   i. All of the above

9. Several studies have been completed regarding the use of testing in the selection process. Schmidt and Hunter (1998) used a variety of tests to determine if any of the several tests had high validity for determining employee potential. General intelligence test, assessment center methods, work sample, integrity test, and combinations of these tests were studied. Which test or combination of tests received the highest validity rating of 0.65?
   a. General Intelligence Test (prediction for managers)
   b. General Intelligence Test (for jobs with average demands)
   c. Assessment Center Methods
   d. General Intelligence Test plus Integrity Test
   e. General Intelligence Test plus Work Sample
   f. All of the above
   g. None of the above

10. The final step in the selection process is to
   a. write a note/letter of thanks to each candidate interviewed;
   b. assess the selection process in terms of accomplished purposes and benefits received;
   c. send a note of appreciation to each person that served as a reference for the candidate that was ultimately selected;
   d. complete the evaluation form for each person that served on the selection committee;
   e. All of the above.

11. School boards now have the authority to delegate the official hiring of a new employee to the school superintendent or to the human resources director. ____True or ____False
12. Empirical evidence indicates that forty out of every one hundred employee applications contain false or questionable information. ____ True or ____False
13. The question "Did the position assignment match with your professional strengths and interests?" would be most appropriate to ask an employee
   a. during the first telephone interview with a position applicant;
   b. in an exit interview;
   c. in relation to his or her previous work or last teaching position;
   d. during a mentor/mentee meeting.

14. One primary difference between hiring a classified employee and a certificated employee is that questions relating to communication skills, working relationships, and continued development are less necessary and less relevant for classified personnel. ____True or ____False

15. Finalization of the employment of any person becomes official when the school board has taken action to approve the appointment. ____True or ____False

Answers to the Pre-Quiz

Answer to question 1 is f, question 2 is false, answer to question 3 is d, answer to question 4 is c, answer to question 5 is d, answer to question 6 is d, question 7 is false, answer to question 8 is h, answer to question 9 is d, answer to question 10 is b, question 11 is false, question 12 is true, answer to question 13 is b, question 14 is false, question 15 is false.

Scoring Results

Your Score

15–13 You are top drawer *****
12–10 You are next to the top drawer ****
9–7 You are in the middle drawer ***
6–4 You are near the top of the bottom drawer **
3–1 You are still in the dresser but in the bottom drawer *
0 Sorry, they put you in the laundry

Discussion of the Pre-Quiz

1. The answer to Question 1, an effective selection process can serve the school and school district in many ways, is f, "improve all of the above." Changes in personnel can facilitate positive changes in the school's program practices. New talent holds the potential of fostering needed innovations in problem solving and decision making. New hires can bring about new employee bonding and retraining activities. Upgrading of instruction and improvements in student achievement are potential pluses. Refreshed relationships can evolve resulting in improved school climate. An improved school climate can lead to improved student academic achievement.
2. Question 2, "An effective selection process is an indefinite endeavor since we have yet to find a way to determine the characteristics of great teachers and how to determine such characteristics in advance of hiring," is false. The affective characteristics of great teachers include caring/loving, effective communication skills, enthusiasm, fairness, sense of humor, good listener and being able to promote a positive climate in his or her classroom.

    Cognitive characteristics of great teachers include teaching knowledge, high test scores, expectation of high standards/goals, quality preparation, organization skills, effective teaching strategies, monitoring of student learning, and motivation of students. Instruments are readily available for determining affective characteristics such as empathy, listening, innovation, focus, and individualized perception (Clifton & Nelson, 1992).

3. The answer to Question 3, "A school board policy related to the hiring of personnel," is d, sets forth the primary purposes/aims of the hiring process as opposed to the administrative procedures necessary for implementing the policy. A school policy is a comprehensive statement of decisions, principles or courses of action that serve toward the achievement of stated goals. Only the school board can adopt the policy. It is equivalent to legislation and related to the question, What to do? On the other hand, an administrative regulation is related to the question, How to do? It is a precise statement calling for specific interpretation and execution.

    The terms policy, regulation, law, rule/procedure and by-law are commonly misused by professional educators. School administrators and teachers are often referring to "our policy" for a matter that in reality is a school procedure. The fact that school policies and administrative regulations are developed by outside agencies militates against reaching a correct understanding of these important terms and their application in school governance.

4. The answer to Question 4, "Which of the following is the best source for defining the behavioral characteristics to be used for rating of position candidates?" is c, the position description for the job in question. A comprehensive position description will include the specific position responsibilities and the related knowledge and skills required for the position, specific qualifications, experience, degrees/licensure and preparation, administrative requirements, and other affective and cognitive qualities for successful position achievement.

5. The answer to Question 5, "Which characteristic ranked 1 of twenty-one characteristics named in one study by principals as being most important for teacher selection data?" is d, "respect for students." None of the other entries ranked better than 12 ("effective discipline"). Following the most important characteristic of respect for students were honesty, ability to work with peers, verbal communication, and quality of previous experience. Most surprising, perhaps, were the choices of ability to assess pupil progress and understanding of subject matter, which ranked 9 and 16 respectively (Norton, 2015).

6. The answer to Question 6, " Which entry below best describes the purposes of an interview guide?" is d. It gives directions/procedures for assessing the criteria relative to each position opening and provides guidelines for specific questions to be used in the interview. An interview guide enhances continuity in the interview by helping each interviewer focus on the selection criteria for the position in question. Inexperienced interviewers

find an interview guide of special value since it supports objectivity on the part of the interviewer as opposed to subjective judgments.

7. Question 7, "TASS refers to 'teacher affective, scholarship and socialization' characteristics," is false. TASS is the Talent Attraction and Selection System. Its focus is on the description of several different approaches for the selection and interviewing of position candidates. The short interview, long interview, and group interview were discussed previously in chapter 3. The TASS interview strategies point out that an interview, depending on its purposes, might be as short as a five-minute telephone call or be planned for as long as two to six hours.

8. The answer to Question 8, "Which of the below entries is not a recognized interview technique used by school districts in the hiring process?" is h, the water boarding interview. All other entries are bona fide interview strategies. Each was discussed previously in chapter 3.

9. The answer to Question 9, "Which test or combination of tests received the highest validity rating of 0.65" [for purposes of employee selection]? is d, a General Intelligence Test plus Integrity Test. We discussed selection testing briefly in chapter 3. Schmidt and Hunter (1998) completed research on the predictability of future job success through testing. Six variations of testing were examined and a performance/success statistic calculated. Table 4.1 shows the results.

10. The answer to Question 10, "The final step in the selection process," is to b, "assess the selection process in terms of accomplished purposes and benefits received." The effectiveness of the recruitment process, for example, should include a statistical examination of the original recruitment pool numbers and the actual number of applicants that remained in the pool for candidate pool selection. How many persons from the candidate pool remained in the pool for hiring consideration? How many in the candidate pool were actually hired and then remained in their position for a second year?

11. Question 11, "School boards now have the authority to delegate the official hiring of a new employee to the school superintendent or to the human resources director," is false. Although school boards have given

Table 4.1. Assessing Job Success Through Testing

Type of Test Administered	Performance/Success Statistic
General Intelligence Test plus Integrity Test	0.65
General Intelligence Test plus Work Sample	0.63
General Intelligence Test (for Managers)	0.58
General Intelligence Test plus Assessment Center Methods	0.53
General Intelligence Test (Jobs with Average Demands)	0.51
Assessment Center Methods	0.37

local school leaders the authority to offer positions contingent on the official approval of the school board and results of background checks, we know of no state that has given hiring approval to any local person or personnel officer. School boards are extensions of the state legislative and therefore have legislative authority to adopt school district policy.

12. Question 12, "Empirical evidence indicates that forty out of every one hundred employee applications contain false or questionable information," is true. This finding shows why application screening is so important. Application screening is a procedure used to determine if applicants do have the qualifications required for the position opening. Such violations have included cases whereby the applicant/candidate did not hold the necessary degree or licensure necessary for the position, did not report his or her record of criminal activities, or included false information regarding work experience.

13. The answer to Question 13 is b. Specific attempts to learn why an employee is leaving your school is important. If asked at the appropriate time, the response might be something that could yet be overturned. Leaving education? More money elsewhere? Poor supervisory relationships? Family reasons? Career opportunity? Burned out?

14. The answer to Question 14, "One primary difference between hiring a classified employee and a certificated employee is that questions relating to communication skills, working relationships, and continued development are less necessary and less relevant for classified personnel," is false. In fact, it is common for the qualification of skill in both verbal and written communication to be on all classified position opening announcements. Staff development training programs for classified employees list such classes as communication skills, conflict management, listening skills, English and grammar, writing for results, leadership skills, team building, workplace courtesy, and valuing diversity in their training programs. Interpersonal relationships also loom important.

15. The answer to Question 15, "Finalization of the employment of any person becomes official when the school board has taken action to approve the appointment," is false. A contract of employment also requires the signature of the new hire. In addition, final approval of employment is contingent on the results of the background check. Once again, the background check looms important.

THE SCHOOL PRINCIPAL AS A HUMAN RESOURCES ADMINISTRATOR

Changes in the administrative function of human resources are witnessed in the increasing practice of delegating additional HR responsibilities to school principals. The school principal is now more directly involved in the recruiting, re-recruiting, selection, development, and orientation of new personnel. HR processes such as staff orientation have become an essential responsibility of local school leaders. *Staff orientation* is the comprehensive complex of activities designed to gain congruency between institutional objectives and position needs. It begins with the position application, continues through job candidacy, hiring, and position placement for as long as the employee and school leaders view it as necessary.

Pre-orientation is those activities provided during the period between the initial contact with the school district and the time the candidate assumes an assignment in the school system. *Getting to Know Us* is a general theme for the pre-orientation. The nature of the school community, the school's mission and vision statements, the career opportunities that are provided to employees by the school district for professional and career development, and other support systems within the district are among the pre-orientation activities.

Post-employment orientation for personnel focuses on providing for effective and efficient transition of personnel into specific roles, including the work environment, personal assistance relative to material and supply sources for instruction, student information, disciplinary practices, student grading procedures, and the initiation of mentoring services.

The orientation process serves several key purposes that (1) encourages talented persons to apply in the school district, (2) assures an effective transition of new district personnel, (3) fosters an understanding of the school and school district's vision and mission statements, (3) reduces or removes potential problems that inhibit work effectiveness, (4) acquaints the employee with the school and community, (5) ascertains and attends to the specific needs of the new employee, (6) re-introduces and identifies the human and physical resources available to the employee, and (7) provides information and guides of information that promote student learning/achievement.

AN ORIENTATION OPERATIONAL MODEL

An effective orientation program necessitates effective planning, coordination, implementation, and evaluation/assessment. Five steps are important for meeting the purposes of the process.

Step 1. The governing board must adopt policies that commit the school district to an effective orientation process and what it is to accomplish. A school board policy serves to underscore the importance of orientation activities and the need for accountable program results.

Step 2. Information is gathered from exit interviews, recent orientation program results, and personnel leaders that will assist in identifying orientation program purposes and needs. Action plans are determined cooperatively by the HR director, school principal, department heads, grade school leaders, and classified job leaders; responsibilities are assigned. Action plans are reviewed in relation to the school board's orientation policy. An action plan serves to guide the human resources director's intentions. It is flexible enough to be revised as successes and perhaps failures are witnessed. Without an action plan, performance is ruled by day-to-day events.

Step 3. Previously determined action plans are implemented. Communication is enhanced, responsibilities are reviewed, and program outcomes are evaluated as fit the case.

Step 4. Orientation programs are monitored, evaluated, and assessed. Hard data that serve for program accountability are collected. Specific means for assessing the orientation results against stated purposes are necessary. What improvements in employee practices were actually realized after the completion of the orientation program(s)?

Step 5. Collected orientation program data are assessed in terms of what went especially well and what improvements/changes are needed? The point is this: are the program efforts that were implemented and the program expenditures that were budgeted actually serving the original program purposes and needs? If so, what hard data serve as evidence of this accomplishment?

HUMAN RESOURCES

Orientation—Certificated and Classified Employees

Orientation of new certificated and classified personnel will be a cooperative activity of the human resources unit, school facilities director, and local school principals. However, orientation is viewed as an ongoing process and is continued as long as the employee and supervisory staff view it as necessary. The next section lists the orientation responsibilities that will be implemented, through cooperative planning and designing activities, at each local school and other offices and facilities within the school district.

School Building Basis

The principal is responsible for the orientation of new certificated and classified employees in his or her school. Principals are expected to give information and general directions in regard to the following activities and services:

1. The organization of the school district's instructional program, supervisory support, instructional resources, school community culture, office

and cafeteria personnel and services, technological support, and other special services available to employees.

2. Instructional resources, including courses of study, curriculum guides, textbooks and supplementary materials, instructional technology, student grading procedures, discipline expectations, maintenance procedures, and related instructional support.

3. The school district's and school's vision and mission statements and their utilization in the provision of instructional program goals and objectives.

4. The school district's and local school's employee support programs in relation to professional and personal needs.

5. The coaching and mentoring services provided within the school district are implemented, and the related professional growth and development activities are made available for classified and professional personnel, including reverse mentoring.

6. A personal conference centering on the employee's position description should be held. The requirements, benefits, clarifications, and bases for implementing performance evaluations and needed revisions/changes in the position specifications should be discussed in detail.

7. Special attention is given to the employee's special interests and talents and how these characteristics can be integrated into the work activities of each individual.

8. Special attention is given to the factor of open communication among teachers, students, administrators, and parents. Teachers and other employees are informed of formal and informal ways of human collaboration. Idea solicitation is ongoing. Every suggestion is considered and acted upon is some manner regardless of its source.

9. Safety regulations are discussed in relation to emergency measures, school intruders, violence, and other troublesome events. Directions for employee actions/responses are discussed and periodically reviewed for the safety of all members of the school staff and its student population.

10. Special sessions are planned and implemented on topics such as performance evaluation, including state and school board requirements, latest research on student learning, accountability of the school staff in relation to student achievement, stated purposes, special accomplishments, and other identified special interests and needs of school personnel.

THE EMPLOYEE ORIENTATION GUIDE

Many school districts nationally have teacher and staff handbooks that serve good purposes relative to informational services and procedures. Increasingly, the *Employee Orientation Guide* is being developed for the orientation of both new and regular employees of the school district. Figure 4.2 includes many of the common information entries in such publications. We do not want to confuse the orientation guide with the school board policy manual. Nevertheless, some topics such as drug-free workplace policy, sexual harassment policy, performance appraisal, negotiations, professional development, sexual harassment, insubordination, and personnel files are common to both documents.

Table of Contents

ARE CURRENT PRACTICES FOR STAFF DEVELOPMENT PRODUCING EXPECTED IMPROVEMENTS?

Teachers commonly have referred to their in-service experiences using such phrases as *sit and get workshops*, *drive-by professional development*, and *here I am, learn me in-service*. The literature is replete with staff development program recommendations, models for implementing staff development, suggestions for developing individual development plans, and essays that focus on the topic of why professional development for teachers and classified personnel is critical.

Most every state in the nation has minimum staff development requirements for non-tenured and tenured teacher personnel. Staff in-service program credits are set forth for classified personnel for moving up the salary scale and becoming eligible for reclassification in a particular job family (Norton, 2008). Yet, the findings of the limited research studies on program results are discouraging at best.

Staff development programs in education have been misdirected in several ways. Doing the same thing that is being done over and over can only result in the same outcomes. Major changes in staff development programs must take place if signs of results are to be seen in reaching best practices, applications of learned material, and related improvements in student achievement. Staff development to be purposeful and long lasting must focus on self-development. It must center on the features of adult learning. It must tie closely to the professional development cycle of the teacher or the individual classified employee.

WHAT HR LEADERS NEED TO KNOW ABOUT ADULT LEARNING

The term *andragogy* stems from the term *pedagogy*. The Greek prefix *peda* refers to a child and the suffix *gogy* (ago) means "to lead: to lead a child." Similarly, the prefix *andro* is "man" and again the suffix *gogy* means "to lead"; together *andragogy* means to "lead man." The contemporary definition of *andragogy* is the methods or techniques used to teach adults. A synthesis of the literature gives us some basic principles important in the teaching/learning of adults. "An understanding of adults and how they learn are as vital to successful adult professional development as the knowledge of children and adolescents at the K-12 level is to their successful learning" (Norton, 2008, p. 216).

As is true with young learners, adults have different learning styles. The term *learning style* refers to how a person learns. Some adults learn best by visual means, whereby pictures, written handouts, films, personal observation, and other means of seeing what is to be learned are most effective. Other adults are auditory learners, and verbal instruction, lectures, listening, and one-on-one instruction works best. Kinesthetic learners learn best by doing something. Hands-on experiences, role playing, skits, and personal involvement in the learning process are necessary. Dare we ask the question relative to how many educational development programs give thought to such adult learning information?

Nevertheless, just knowing about adult learning styles is not sufficient. Consensus of the literature and empirical experience underscore the importance of other relevant principles and practices that are viewed as being necessary for fostering successful learning for adults. If HR leaders fail to consider these factors when planning and implementing professional development for teachers, administrators, and classified employees, the results of their efforts most likely will fail to find a place in practice.

A CONSENSUS OF RECOMMENDATIONS FOR ADULT LEARNING PROGRAMMING

Attempting to rectify "best of the best" development programs that do not result in improved practices is troublesome at best. We do know that just trying to grow somebody by giving him or her something that others believe is important for him or her to know does not meet the need. We repeat that effective growth and development is self-development. In this context, certain basic characteristic for adult learning would appear to be significant. A synthesis of the literature and knowledge gained from empirical experience would lead us to recommend several guidelines for enhancing the effectiveness of our school district's professional development program activities and guiding principles. Such activities and principles include the following:

1. Personal engagement—Unless the adult person sees and understands the need to learn, the objective of self-development cannot be accomplished. We agree with Clifton and Nelson (1992) that people are more apt to soar with their strengths. That is, achievement is realized to a greater extent when the focus is on the strengths rather than on the weaknesses of the individual. Placing emphasis on one's weaknesses possibly could improve performance to a level of mediocrity, but focusing on one's strengths can lead to even higher levels of innovation and achievement.
2. Need to learn—Although the HR director or other supervisor believes that an employee would benefit by increasing his or her knowledge and skill by participating in a certain in-service program, the adult employee needs

to understand why the activity is necessary in his or her line of work. Just why do I need to learn something? Why is the learning important for me to know? What current problems will the development program resolve for me? Relevance to an employee's work serves to foster readiness to learn. Thus, internal motivation rather than external enforcement is the foundation for the employee's self-development.

3. Personal involvement—Empirical evidence supports the fact that adults learn best when they are initially involved and meaningfully informed of the planned development activities. Are the program activities aligned with the individual development plan of the employee? Employees have different learning styles. They prefer to be able to learn according to their own methods. Certainly, adults seek support and guidance in their efforts to improve, but they also appreciate the opportunity to use personal autonomy in selecting improvement methods rather than being told what and how to do something.

4. Learning characteristics—Learning for adults commonly is facilitated when carried out in less structured situations. As noted above, adult learners want to be actively involved as opposed to sitting and listening. Past experience greatly influences adult attitudes toward learning. Past experience serves as a foundation for their involvement and motivation for learning; it must be relevant to current needs and interests. When adults have a key reason for learning, motivation to learn is facilitated. Immediate relevance is the key for readiness to learn.

5. Program accountability—The most effective adult learning is problem centered. Content-centered programs tend to focus on the organization's ideas as to what growth and development are needed on the part of the employees. The result most often in the mind of the participant is, "OK, here I am. Now grow me!" When the employee has had the opportunity to participate in the completion of his or her position analysis and job description, the competent employee believes that it is important to achieve these outcomes. When the outcomes are indeed accomplished, factors like increased self-esteem, increased job satisfaction, personal encouragement, commitment, and positive human relations are fostered.

WHAT CAN BE DONE TO IMPROVE COMMUNICATIONS AMONG STAFF PERSONNEL?

If we need to improve communications, it certainly doesn't mean more committee reports are needed. Federal regulations, school board direction sheets, office forms, memos, e-mails, report forms certainly aren't being rationed. If we need to improve school communication practices, we surely mean better quality and more effectiveness and not an increase in volume. A question for reflection is, "What could we possibly accomplish if by some miracle communication became a cursory and simplistic process whereby individuals came to understand and to appreciate one another's dialogue with consummate precision?" What possible goals would be achieved?

We have to admit that communication problem solutions are both challenging and baffling. No quick and easy ways to develop positive relationships between individuals and groups are available. We face all kinds of human impediments. How people communicate depends upon how they have lived, what they've done, their experiences, and a variety of other factors. Differences exist not just in the sets of fingerprints. Each person thinks, talks, writes, and behaves differently. Nevertheless, the HR director must give special thought to communication. Peter Drucker has stated that effective executives take responsibility for communicating.

"Effective executives make sure that both their action plans and their information need are understood. Specifically, this means that they share their plans with and ask for comments from all colleagues—superiors, subordinates, and peers. At the same time, they let each person know what information they'll need to get the job done. The information flow from subordinate to boss is usually what gets the most attention. But executives need to pay equal attention to peers' and superiors' information needs" (Drucker, 2004, p. 9).

An open-door policy and improved transparency are becoming more important as a strategy for keeping employees on board. This concept centers on increasing the sharing of information that affects the employee's work environment, discussing problems and issues that all too often are kept within the confines of the school district offices, and getting input and feedback from employees on probable program changes, best practices for improvement, and ways to improve the climate in which the employee must serve.

THE IMPACT OF TECHNOLOGICAL SERVICES

Reportedly, 95% of business organizations now use software for payroll, recruitment, and talent management. School district recruiters are able to take advantage of the Internet to both advertise position openings and to gain "position seekers" information advertised by employment agencies. The orientation and training activities of the school district can benefit by use of technology as well. The district can contact large numbers of employees of program information and can also assess employee progress by use of testing programs and personal feedback. Communication matters can be distributed on a wide basis among the school district's employees; feedback can be retrieved expeditiously.

Technology provides the opportunity for the storage of large amounts of data that also becomes readily retrievable. Record keeping becomes more manageable and usable and eliminates a great deal of the manual methods in relation to such activities as accounting and payroll. In addition, technological programs can be installed that serve as *boomerang reminders* for important feedback and/or time alerts for deadlines that must be met.

AM I MAKING MYSELF CLEAR?

A program, idea, or concept will be developed, thought through, clarified, perhaps piloted, evaluated, and finally introduced to the school or school system as a whole for execution. At this point, a whole new array of problems is likely to come into being. Various kinds of misunderstandings become apparent. The "new idea" is cold turkey to many employees unless a planned procedure for follow-up implementation is in place. What is needed to help ameliorate such problems is leadership in developing a culture of participation within the school and school district.

Research has made it clear that any system that is chosen carries with it its own set of problems. The message is read and interpreted differently from level to level and person to person. Various distortions are likely to result. There exists perception distortion, judgment distortion, and action distortion. *Perception distortion* occurs when the person is not fully aware that he or she had misread or misinterpreted the message. *Judgment distortion* occurs when the person believes that he or she interpreted the message incorrectly and the majority did not. *Action distortion* subjects know that they understood the message correctly but were reluctant to be different from an incorrect opinion of the majority.

It is clear, according to behavior research, that an individual tends to "read" a communication as he or she wishes. Additionally, the person is able to shut out what tends to be threatening even to the extent that the message did not really occur. Carefully planned communication is required to fill these human communication gaps.

EFFECTIVE COMMUNICATION

The success of a communications program depends largely on how well the school leaders have been able to define the school system's and school's goals as well as the specific aims of the communication efforts. All of the very best communication objectives cannot help a school that hasn't crystalized its thinking about what it is and where it is going.

Successful communication depends more on the climate of the school than on the number and type of formal media. We contend that the more positive the climate the less is the need for formal media. An open, positive school climate holds a high level of expectation that when a message is sent it will be listened to; that people are in the know; that peoples' opinions are respected and even expected. A pattern of openness and trust generates a good communication climate. Employees in a positive school climate can be well informed even though little formal media are used.

Communication is not complete until there has been some interaction and some feedback has taken place. An individual becomes aware of the effect of a situation on him or her and also has become aware of the effect of his or her effect on the situation. Behavioral scientists tell us that we cannot change behavior by the weight of authority alone. Until the person becomes involved in the process, there is no guarantee that there will be any personal reception of the idea or information. Communication must be personalized to the fullest extent possible. We communicate to an individual and must have a personal impact to be heard.

CHECK PLEASE

Effective follow-up is just as important as the communication itself. Follow-up checks should be made to determine if communications have been received and understood. Communication planning should include the following questions: (1) Are communication routes or channels of appeal defined in the event of misunderstanding, disagreement, or conflict? (2) Are we being alert to communication feedback, pro or con? If no feedback, we ask why. (3) Are there complaints on the volume of communication from the school district, principal's office, and other offices of the school system? Are the channels of communication clearly specified and widely known? Is feedback information given due concern and reported back as fits the case? Are there voluntary reports on breakdowns of communications?

MENTORING AND COACHING STRATEGIES

How many persons at your school do you believe are effective/qualified mentors or coaches? Perhaps the answer to the question depends on what one believes are the purposes of the two roles. What activities does a coach perform and do they differ from those of a qualified mentor? Do either of the roles require special knowledge and skills or are the roles just something that one does to show others "how things are done around here"? We have been told by some new teachers that their mentor simply welcomed them to the school and told them to let them know if they had any questions about anything.

There are important differences between coaching and mentoring. Several important differences are set forth in Table 4.2.

NEW METHODS OF MENTORING

Group mentoring and reverse mentoring are more recent methods of mentoring within school systems and local schools. *Group mentoring* is a strategy

Table 4.2.   Differences between Coaching and Mentoring

The Mentoring Process	The Coaching Process
Refers to the art of helping to steer an individual in the same field.	Uses techniques in a full range of backgrounds and a variety of fields.
Helps one to answer the question "How can I best network?"	Helps the individual to think about "what challenges and problems do I need to address now?"
Focuses on relationships relative to his or her professional and personal success.	Focuses on enhancing current skills.
Centers on personal improvement now and the future.	Centers on current job improvement.
Is planned to determine guidelines for mentoring activities; what is to be accomplished?	Necessitates the support of the individual's current supervisor.
Centers on the actual implementation of the talent development plan of the employee.	Serves to guide and promote progress toward the individual's career and special interests.
Helps in developing talent within the school system.	Helps the individual identify and implement his or her personal strengths.
Can be a powerful stimulus for change and learning; builds such factors as confidence, commitment, and competency.	Is task oriented. It focuses on specific skills such as communication and business management.
Mentoring is an ongoing, long-term process and lasts for as long as nine months to a year. Long as it is, it ends when the coaching experience has been satisfactorily accomplished.	Coaching is short term.
Facilitates the process of succession planning when the school system is interested in improving and developing leadership talent.	Might focus on one specific problem of an individual that is especially troublesome and inhibiting his or her work progress.
Centers on the goals and objectives that the mentee wishes to accomplish. It is development driven. It enhances skills for present and future positions.	Coaching is performance driven. It enhances current or new skills.

for mentoring groups of mentees as opposed to the common one-on-one mentoring strategy. *Reverse mentoring* places a younger employee as the mentor for a person that has been in the school system for a longer period of time. For example, some younger persons are often more skilled and knowledgeable of the technology available to school leaders today.

Group mentoring is important when the number of quality mentors are not available or when it is necessary to reach more people than can be accomplished with one-to-one mentoring strategies. Group mentoring has the potential of improving the collaboration within the school and school district. When school employees are able to *connect*, growth and development are enhanced. In addition, more employees are able to share in the knowledge and skills of a qualified mentor. Some authorities have pointed out that a qualified mentor can encounter burnout in attempts to work one to one with so many different mentees. Zachary (2016) speaks of three approaches to group mentoring: (1) facilitated group mentoring, (2) peer-group mentoring, and (3) team mentoring.

Facilitated group mentoring involves a group of teachers or other school employees that come together to achieve a specific learning goal. The group facilitator keeps the group on track by asking appropriate questions and sharing his or her own experiences as fits the case. Using this strategy, participating members of the group insert their experiences into the discussion and ask questions of the group mentor that enriches the group experience.

Peer-group mentoring puts together a group of school or school district members with similar interests and needs. Thus, the group's agenda centers directly on issues and problems that are being encountered by the group's members. Although the group does not include a special mentor, the collected talents of the group serve to direct the members' questions and input. It is common for the members of the peer group to volunteer to follow up on unanswered questions and report back at the next group session. Participation and personal involvement are important outcomes of peer-group mentoring.

Team mentoring does include a mentor or mentors that work with the group in relation to the accomplishment of mutually determined learning goals and related best practices. The primary focus of the group is centered on learning effective methods and strategies for engaging students in the learning process. Mentors do share their knowledge and skill with the group as fits the case but commonly ask related questions that serve to guide the learning of the team. Team mentoring is cooperative and collaborative. Check Bleedorn's snapshot as related to teamwork, integration, and collaboration.

Chapter Snapshot

Berenice D. Bleedorn (1996) perhaps said it best: "Respect and love for each other; soul of group is ultimate feature in team fabric" (p. 1). Bleedorn references her experience in listening to a jazz trio, saxophonist, guitarist, and bassist, who were entertaining at a Sunday brunch. After the trio established the melody or theme of the song being played, each member of the trio played a solo that improvised and elaborated on the melody while the other two players played support. Bleedorn wondered whether the demonstration of teamwork of the trio could be analyzed as it applied to the search for team-building strategies in other places.

The question arose as to just how the trio so ably integrated themselves into a positive team product. The answer was that first and foremost you listen carefully to the other players and are responsive; you share the leadership. When another member takes a solo, you support and encourage him or her. You listen to everyone else and be supportive. If teams in the workplace could relate their task to the jazz process, their guidelines would probably go something like this: (1) Listen to everyone else. Be supportive. (2) Be sensitive to the moods of others. (3) Trust your intuition. (4) Risk expressing your ideas. (5) Be playful, lighten up, and think smart. (6) Be open to new experiential patterns and directions. (7) Bring the outside world into the picture; think systematically. Mutual respect and love for each other and for the shared musical soul of the group is the ultimate feature and the fabric of the team (Bleedorn, 1996, November 11).

Reverse mentoring is typified by having a younger, more junior employee serve as the mentor for a senior, more experienced member of the organization. In this way, it gives the senior member an opportunity to keep up to date with the latest trends and technological innovations that commonly are possessed by technology-savvy millennials (Manson, 2015). As underscored by Manson, reverse mentoring gives credibility to the fact that younger members of the organization have something to teach and senior members must always keep learning. The younger mentor benefits from the senior member's knowledge and experience by gaining a better understanding of the overall issues facing contemporary organizations.

The senior member and the organization benefit by increasing employee retention and fostering the development of younger talent within the system. "Reverse mentoring is an innovative use of mentoring. It emphasizes the idea that learning never stops while supporting the idea that the young have something to teach, which is why we see so much interest around it" (Manson, 2015, p. 1).

How does one get started on a program of reverse mentoring? It could be as simple as asking a new first-year teacher a help question. "Sara, we need some ideas as to how we can use our communication media to communicate more effectively with our parents. What ideas might you suggest?" or "Mark, someone mentioned to me that new young teachers always have something to teach experienced employees. Do you agree with that contention?" One never quite knows where such questions might lead, but reverse mentoring certainly is a potential outcome.

Authorities do have recommendations that serve to facilitate the success of various methods of reverse mentoring. In regard to reverse mentoring, the common recommendations include the need to do the following: (1) Give special attention to matching mentors and mentees. Consider the characteristic of good social skills. Empirical evidence has revealed that most every individual want to do a better job even though they might act as though improvement for them is not needed. When these persons get involved and their ideas are discussed objectively, their involvement increases in a positive direction. (2) Develop an informal positive relationship. Avoid viewing the reverse mentoring process as the boss and the new kid on the block. Rather, the two parties must be able to interact as important employees that can make a difference in their work performance and therefore in the school system. (3) Set goals of mutual interest and concern. How will the reverse mentoring sessions benefit both parties? How will it benefit the school or school system? Keep the mentoring goals in mind but retain an informal setting that encourages creative give and take. Avoid what is viewed as one-upmanship.

Reverse mentoring above all else must be an enjoyable venture. Older mentees comment about other benefits of reverse learning. For example, senior mentees commonly learn to hold back rather than always jump into a conversation. It brings the skill of listening into play but with a different perspective. The senior learns to see things from a different point of view.

THE PERFORMANCE EVALUATION AND ASSESSMENT PROCESSES

Most states continue to implement state and school board requirements for teacher performance evaluations. In addition, it has become more common for local school principals to be directly involved in the performance evaluations of classified employees under their supervision. There is no question about the time that is required to complete performance evaluations. A thorough teacher performance includes orientation activities to the evaluation plan, pre-classroom observation conferencing, scheduled classroom observation, completion of the observation report, post-observation conferencing, and follow-up activities relative to the individual's improvement plan.

Classroom performance evaluations come under two classifications: formative and summative. A *formative evaluation* focuses on purposes related to performance improvement. On the other hand, a *summative evaluation* focuses on employment continuation, dismissal, or decisions relative to merit pay. In the case of classified personnel, a summative evaluation commonly is required for consideration of job grade improvement.

Although states have set forth legislation that requires people that are evaluating teachers to be qualified to do so, research evidence has yet to tie performance evaluation to the matter of improvements in student achievement. We tend to take for granted that the in-service program for lesson plan development or for student engagement in learning will be implemented in practice and result in improved teacher performance. This assumption has encouraged school leaders to turn to other staff improvement strategies, including coaching and mentoring. Mentoring is viewed as a more personalized strategy for developing talent.

Authorities argue that mentoring serves to engage employees by helping them to develop knowledge and skills that are needed to move ahead in their career path. In this sense, the organization is being active in developing its own talent. The mentor serves a personal service by helping the mentee develop competency in his or her personal professional career pursuits. Effective mentoring is an important activity in the overall process of performance management.

TRENDING TOWARD PERFORMANCE MANAGEMENT

Performance management differs from performance evaluation. *Performance evaluation* is the process of determining how well the employee is performing relative to the specific goals, objectives, and standards established for the position. Thus, an observation of a teacher's classroom performance by the school principal represents a performance evaluation or appraisal. On the other hand, performance management includes the variety of activities that the human resources administrator utilizes to determine the extent to which the goals and standards of a position are being met.

Performance management is the process of creating a work environment in which people are enabled to perform to the best of their abilities. How is such a work environment established? Employees need to be informed and must have feedback on job purposes and standards. Job descriptions, performance standards, and continuous feedback on performance evaluations are important activities in performance management. We submit that the first four chapters of this book have emphasized many of the human resources processes that serve as the foundation for effective performance management.

These processes include the following: the development of clear and meaningful job descriptions, planning and implementing effective processes of recruitment and re-recruitment, programming effective selection methods, establishing purposeful orientation activities, administering high-quality coaching and mentoring strategies, giving recognition for quality work results, providing a variety of activities for professional growth and development, establishing meaningful opportunities for employees to advance career-wise within the school district, and utilizing informational strategies such as exit interviews to learn more about the effectiveness of the school and school district's strengths and areas that need to be improved.

A relatively new term has emerged within the human resources function. We have known about the benefits of exit interviews for many years. But why wait until after an employee decides to sever relationships with the school system to learn why he or she is leaving? At that time, there often is little or nothing that you can do to change the employee's mind. *Stay interviews* are being implemented to learn what it would take for an employee to stay with the school system. What is motivating the employee to stay with the school system? What might be done to create a more attractive work environment?

A school principal or HR director cannot expect to interview every employee each year. Perhaps you should begin with employees that have been with you for the longest period of time and also have contributed positively to the school and school district's goals and objectives by performing strongly in their work positions.

Knowing the reasons for losing personnel serves the primary purpose of assessing what might be done to obviate the situation. The state of Texas completed an exit report centering on the reasons that employees were leaving the state agencies voluntarily. Although fifteen different reasons for leaving were identified, the reasons of retirement (26.4%), better pay/benefits (20%), poor working conditions/environment (12.3%), issues with their supervisor/employees (8.6%), personal or family health (7.3%), and no or little career advancement opportunities (6.9%) led the listing of reasons for leaving. Only 1.2% listed relationships with coworkers as a reason for leaving.

Take a moment to review the foregoing reasons for leaving. Ask yourself what provisions, steps, changes, programs, or counseling might be implemented to ameliorate the inferred issues/problems stated as reasons for resigning from the state agencies. For example, consider the leading reason of retirement. Minimally, what might be done to retain a number of the voluntary retirements? What, if anything, might the organization do to keep talented potential retirees on the job? Might some of the retirees be available for part-time work? Is there a possibility that they would be interested in returning to work after a period of time off? How might you find out? You ask them!

Consider the reason of poor working conditions/environment as a reason for leaving. Heathfield (2016) views performance management as a process of creating a positive work environment that enhances the ability of each employee to perform at his or her highest level of competency. The process begins at the outset of the recruiting process and is carried on continuously through effective selection, orientation, placement, and development processes and the position responsibilities of the worker.

In addition, several features of personnel management must be in place: (1) The purposes of the job/position must be clearly set forth in a position description. (2) Performance goals or standards are determined for the position. Goals or standards must be clearly defined with measurable outcomes. (3) Position goals or standards must be prioritized and standards must be clear. (4) Collaboration between the employee and supervisor must be ongoing with give and take feedback that results in a consensus outcome. (5) Keeping a record of meeting reports, special work outcomes, and issues/problems that were encountered and resolved or remain standing is essential. (6) Obtaining input from other sources, including coworkers, parents, students (as fits the case), fosters cooperation. (7) Establishing an effective mentoring and coaching program for promoting the employee's interest and needs or developing the individual's individual development plan serves positive purposes.

FOSTERING EMPLOYMENT ENGAGEMENT

Culture has been defined within the business sector as the sense of how things are done around here. *Employee engagement*, on the other hand, is how employees feel about how things are done around here (Brown et al., 2016). Engagement looms important since it is a measure of the school system's health and a key window into the potential future issues and the employees' support for change. Each of these factors must be clearly set forth in the position description of the school district's human resources director. Engagement includes such factors as meaningful work, trust, collaboration, appreciation, and opportunities for growth.

THE PERFORMANCE AND EVALUATION PROCESS: COOPERATING WITH LOCAL SCHOOL PERSONNEL

One human resources director commented that "it's somewhat strange that a mathematics teacher applicant looks so much better in August just before school starts than he or she did when the applicant was first interviewed in early April." The remaining position openings in August do seem to make the need for hiring someone for unfilled positions change one's perspective. In the same way, we cannot help believe that the accountability for teacher performance evaluations changes with the existing number of available candidates. Please do not stop reading, however, because this situation is discussed in more depth in a later section of the chapter.

The presence of state statutes mandating teacher performance evaluations will, of course, require the continuation of teacher performance evaluations and assessments. The next section of the chapter discusses the importance of planning, designing, and implementing successful performance evaluations.

PERSONNEL MANAGEMENT IN A LEGAL WORLD

The presence of legal implications for human resources activities are prevalent in every HR processes. A comprehensive coverage of the legal considerations facing HR directors and school principals is beyond the scope of this chapter. For an in-depth coverage of the law encountered by school principals, we recommend the book *The Legal World of the School Principal* published by Rowman & Littlefield in 2016 authored by Norton. We have been given permission by Rowman & Littlefield to present one ruling by the United States Supreme Court case that was presented in the aforementioned book on the matter of due rights and background checks.

CLEVELAND BOARD V. LOUDERMILL (U.S. SUPREME COURT, 1981–1986, 470 U.S. 532, 1985). DUE PROCESS RIGHTS

It is common for schools today to require background checks as a hiring procedure. In the case of Loudermill, he was hired as a security guard, and after hiring it was discovered that he had lied on his application about never having been convicted of a felony. Since Loudermill has been hired, by state statute, he had retained curtained property rights. The board did grant him a review, but not until after nine months of his termination. Loudermill argued that his rights had been violated since he did not have an opportunity to defend himself before being terminated and that his firing was in violation of the due process rights of the Fourteenth Amendment.

Two other courts considered the case and decided that the board had violated Loudermill's due process rights. Ultimately, the case went to the Supreme Court. The Court ruled an 8 to 1 vote that the answer to the question "Can a state remove a civil servant's rights to employment before providing an opportunity to respond to the charges?" was no. Due process before termination is not only required but also it is in the best interests of the employees and not a significant administrative burden for the employing agency. The due process of the Fourteenth Amendment required a hearing, and it should be concluded in a meaningful time. The rights and interests of the employee outweighed the state's interests in quickly dismissing employees (Norton, 2016).

According to Rossmiller and others (1978), there appears to be no question concerning the school board's authority to establish reasonable policies and regulations for the purpose of promoting professional growth and development on the part of employees. Such policies automatically are a part of the teacher's contract. In addition, the school board can set growth expectations even higher than those set by the state within reason. Following *Magenheim v. Board of Education of School District of Riverview Gardens*, teachers also may be required to join one or more teacher associations, local, state, or national, as a condition for enjoying benefits of professional value to the teacher and to the school system (Case 347 S. W. 2nd 409, Mo. 1961).

Key Chapter Ideas and Recommendations

- Effective hiring can reduce the need, time, and costs for "remediation" improvement programs. However, personnel growth and development will continue to loom significant in school improvement practices due primarily to the nature of ongoing societal change.
- The orientation process is much more that a three-day period of time set aside to get ready for opening day. Effective employee orientation is a pre- and post-process that begins when a potential employee completes a position application and continues for as long as the employee and school personnel view it as necessary. The school board must adopt an official policy that establishes the aims and leadership for the orientation process, and the HR unit must establish procedures and accountability measures for its results.
- Employee orientation and growth and development activities to be effective must be tuned to the characteristics of adult learning. The factors of employee need, interest, and involvement are required contingencies. The concept of self-development is recommended. Growth and development are not something that the leader does to or for someone; rather, growth takes place most effectively when the adult learner sees the need for self-engagement in meeting the ongoing changes in the work environment.
- School climate, without question, is one of the human resources unit's primary tasks. HR directors must work closely with local school principals in the implementation of what we now know about improving the climate of the school. New looks at the communication process in the school district and schools are of paramount importance. Improvements must focus on the leaders' ability to define clearly the goals of the school district and the vital importance of each position in serving to achieve these goals.
- Effective coaching and mentoring can achieve successful ends that have evaded positive results previously. Excessive time and resources being spent on classroom teacher evaluations need close attention. In spite of state and local school board requirements for ongoing performance evaluations,

positive evidence of student achievement results is missing. The growing dimensions of coaching and mentoring along with greater attention to performance management strategies auger well for improved school practices.

Discussion Questions

1. To our knowledge, the first book ever published in personnel management was titled *Personnel Administration* (Teach & Metcalf, 1920). The National Society for the Study of Education in 1958 published a book titled *Personnel Services in Education*. Currently, the term *human resources* has replaced the term *personnel*. Here are a few of the other term changes in this area of education. *Induction* to *orientation*, *personnel management* to *human resources administration*, *training* to *development*, *discharge* to *dismissal*, *esprit de corps* to *morale*, *collective bargaining* to *professional negotiation*.

    In small groups or individually, give consideration to the several word/concept changes that have taken place over the years. Are you able to give some rationale as reasons for these changes? For example, we might suggest that trending respect for the individual worker can be seen in the changes (e.g., personnel management vs. human resources administration).

2. Give consideration to your school district's orientation activities or to a school with which you are most familiar. To what extent do the orientation activities compare and/or include those set forth in this chapter?

3. Most laymen will have some understanding of teacher evaluation, in-service development, and organizational climate. However, a school board member asks you about the term *performance management*. Write a paragraph or two that encompasses the response that you give the board member.

4. Consider your current employment or the educational position that you most likely will enter in the next few years. If a reverse mentoring program were implemented in the institution in which you are or will be employed, list several specific topics, skills, or talent areas that you could contribute as either a mentor or the reverse mentor?

CASE STUDIES

Case 4.1   I Know I Have a Program That's Good for Them

Merlin George had just completed his first year as principal of Southeast High School. George was hired after serving for five years as assistant principal in another high school in the Wymore School District. During his first year at Southeast, Principal George spent considerable time getting to know the school staff and students. He worked with the school district's human resources director in the implementation of a new 360-degree employee performance evaluation program whereby performance feedback was received from a full circle of one's supervisors, subordinates, clients, and others with whom the employee interacts. The evaluation program received praise from all sources involved.

Principal George also had worked on an orientation/in-service program that he wanted to implement at Southeast High School during the following year. The growth and development program was based on the performance needs as determined by the performance evaluation outcomes of the past school year. Feedback from evaluators in the 360-degree employee performance program was based on a rating scale of 1 (low) to 5 (high) for each criterion being rated. Thus, the orientation/in-service activities for George's program would include activities that had received low scores below the rating of 3.

George met with the school district's HR director, Sharon Lloy, to explain his program to her and to gain her support for its implementation.

"This program centers on the real needs of our professional teachers and also demonstrates our accountability in paying attention to performance outcomes," stated Principal George. "It also would show our parents, students, and others who work with our teaching staff that their input is appreciated. I don't see why teachers from the three other high schools in the district couldn't participate in the program as well. With your OK, I would like to move ahead on this project and be prepared to put it into place sometime after the first six weeks of school next year."

Discussion Exercise

Assume the role of Sharon Lloy, HR director, and write out your response to Principal George's program request. Be as specific as possible in your response by avoiding answers such as "I will think about it" or "There are other in-service program plans at this time." It is certain that considerable time for planning such an activity and provisions for the needed resources to implement such a program would be important considerations. Rather, think more about the activity itself, its rationale and related purposes. Give consideration to the information discussed in this chapter and how this information would support or not support the in-service program as recommended by George.

REFERENCES

Bleedorn, B. D. (1996, November 11). For lesson in teamwork, try listening to some jazz. *Business Forum.* Minneapolis, MN: Star Tribune.

Bloss, J. M. (1882). *Thirteenth report of the superintendent of public instruction of the state of Indiana to the governor: State of Indiana.* Superintendent of Public Instruction, State of Indiana Received December 11, 1882, examined by the Governor, and delivered to the Secretary of State to be filed and preserved in his office, published as may be ordered by the Commissioner of Public Printing. Frank H. Blackstone, Secretary of State.

Brown, D., Bersin, J., Gosling, G., & Sloan, L. (2016, February 29). *Engagement: Always on.* New York: Deloitte University Press.

Clifton, D. O., & Nelson, P. (1992). *Soar with your strengths.* New York: Dell.

Drucker, P. F. (2004, June). What makes an effective executive. *Harvard Business Review: Communication.* From the Web: https://hbr.org/2004/06/what-makes-an-effective-executive

Heathfield, S. M. (2016). *Performance management.* From the Web: http://thebalance. com/performance_appraisals_dont_work_1918846

Manson, M. (2015, March 16). *Modern mentoring: Reverse mentoring.* From the Web: http://chronus.com/blog/reverse/mentoring

Norton, M. S. (2008). *Human resources administration for educational leaders.* Thousand Oaks, CA: Sage.

Norton, M. S. (2015). *The principal as human resources leader: A guide to exemplary practices for personnel administration.* New York: Routledge.

Norton, M. S. (2016). *The legal world of the school principal: What leaders need to know about school law.* Lanham, MD: Rowman & Littlefield.

Peterson, L. J., Rossmiller, R. A., & Volz, M. M. (1978). *The law and public school operation.* San Francisco, CA: Harper & Row.

Tead, O., & Metcalf, H. C. (1920). *Personnel Administration.* New York: McGraw-Hill Book Company, Inc.

Schmidt, F. L., & Hunter, J. F. (1998). The validity and utility of selection methods in personnel psychology: Practical and theoretical implications of 85 years of research findings. *Psychological Bulletin,* 124, 262–274.

Zachary, L. J. (2016, May 320). *Group mentoring: Strategies for success in group mentoring.* From the Web: http://wiley.com/wileyCDA/wileytitle/productcd-047090772x.html

Chapter 5

The Working World of the Classified Staff

Primary chapter goal: To present the comprehensiveness of the responsibilities of classified personnel in their support role toward the achievement of the school district's goals and objectives.

Classified or *support personnel* are all of the school district employees who hold positions not requiring certification. However, certain classified positions do require considerable preparation and licensure for employment in school districts. It is common to find fifteen or more different *job families* for classified personnel in school districts today. Within each major job family, there are many appropriately graded employee positions. Specific positions within job families do vary among school districts nationally due primarily to differences in student enrollments, program offerings, school locations, and special service needs within school districts.

Percentage estimates for the number of classified personnel in school districts vary from 30% to 60%. In a school district with a total staff of 750 employees, 225 to 450 are likely to be classified employees, who lend strong supportive services toward the goals and objectives of the school district. How certain central office positions in school districts are classified for certification purposes tends to vary among the states.

We often think of classified personnel job classifications under the four titles of secretarial/clerical, maintenance, food service, and fiscal business operations. However, the job family of fiscal business operations commonly includes many employee jobs, such as executive director of budget and finance, accounting manager, accounting clerk, budget coordinator, director of finance, payroll clerk, and purchasing agent, none of which is a certificated position.

We examined the job descriptions for each of the foregoing positions in the Boyd County Public Schools of Ashland, Kentucky (Boyd County Public School District, 2001). Each comprehensive job description included information such as position qualifications, physical requirements, and job goals and objectives. In addition, each of the individual job positions sets forth ten or more general duties and performance responsibilities, for example, "shall strive to maintain and improve professional competence" and "shall work to develop a positive public relationship between home and school."

Give thought to the other job families of classified personnel that commonly exist in school systems today. The point here is the fact that every classified job family is founded on a related group of positions that require specific knowledge and skills that support the purposes of the school district in important ways.

One school district in Kentucky has eleven different position levels under the code for secretarial/clerical employees at the school district office level. The position levels include secretary to the superintendent, administrative secretary/assistant I, administrative secretary/assistant II, administrative secretary/assistant II-office manager, administrative secretary/assistant II-special education, administrative secretary/assistant II-superintendent, school secretary, staff support secretary, clerical assistant III, clerical assistant II, and receptionist. It is quite possible, of course, that jobs in two different school districts are quite similar but only have different position titles.

In small- to medium-sized school districts, it is quite common for the human resources director to administer both classified and certificated staff personnel. Best estimates indicate that 75% of practicing HR directors are responsible for both certificated and classified personnel. Due to the expanded employee numbers in larger school districts today, separate HR directors for classified and certificated personnel have become more common. As explained in previous chapters of the book, the HR processes of recruiting, selection, placement, orientation, and others for certificated and classified employees are similar. That is, classified personnel must be recruited, interviewed, and hired using procedures quite similar to those for certificated personnel.

The comprehensiveness of position descriptions for classified personnel are somewhat surprising to those who are not familiar with the work that these employees perform. The following position description for a food service manager is a case in point. The position description is not presented as a model for all school districts but rather as an example of a classified employee job position in one school district (Boyd County Public Schools District, Ashland, KY). Read the following position description and consider its clarity and specificity. For example, how might entries #1 and #2 under job qualifications and #1, #6, #7 and #9 under general duties and performance responsibilities be more specifically expressed?

Take a moment to think about what entry 1 under General Duties and Performance Responsibilities (Selected) really means in the following position description for a food service manager. Does it refer to school board policies or to established administrative regulations of the school district? Or might it be a guideline for the position as established by the food service manager's supervisor? Position descriptions necessarily must be sufficiently comprehensive but they also must be clear. Courts have ruled that the position description of an employee is an extension of his or her contractual agreement.

Position Description

TITLE: Food Service Manager Assigned School Site
APPOINTMENT: A food service manager shall be appointed annually, upon the recommendation of the school district director of human resources, director of food service, and local school principal; a hiring recommendation is sent to the school superintendent.

Job Qualifications

1. Must be able to communicate effectively both orally and in writing with parents, students, and faculty.
2. Must possess and demonstrate people skills within a team-oriented environment.
3. Must have obtained a high school diploma or GED.
4. Must have a minimum of three years of experience in food service operations within a school setting.
5. Must complete the training course for school food service personnel as prescribed by state statutes.

Physical Requirements

Must have the physical ability to perform all body movements required by the job description. No discrimination shall be given in case of special needs personnel who can demonstrate that they have the abilities needed to be effective in the position.

JOB GOAL: To manage and coordinate the day-to-day food service operations of an assigned school site; assure compliance with district, state, and federal requirements and laws regarding nutrition, sanitation, safety, and record keeping; select, assign, schedule, supervise, direct, and evaluate food service personnel.

General Duties and Performance Responsibilities (Selected)

1. Determine appropriate action within clearly defined guidelines.
2. Present a positive image of the school to the parents, and convey to them the school's genuine concern with the education, growth, and development of each student.
3. Seek to establish friendly and cooperative partnerships between home and school.
4. Work to develop a positive public relationship between the school district and the community.
5. Carry out assignments in a timely manner without undue checking.
6. React positively to directives.
7. Have a willingness to cooperate with the superintendent, district administrators, principals, and staff.
8. Maintain and improve professional competence.
9. Take necessary precautions to protect students, equipment, materials, and facilities.
10. Maintain the confidentiality, both verbally and in written form, of each student's educational records.
11. Adhere to School Board of Education policies and procedures.

Specific Duties and Performance Responsibilities

1. Manage, coordinate, and oversee the day-to-day food service operations at an assigned school site.
2. Compare menus, assuring compliance with regulations and requirements.
3. Estimate and order amount of food and supplies needed for operations.
4. Monitor and control expenditures.
5. Maintain an assigned budget.
6. Assist in the selection of food service employees.
7. Direct, assign, schedule, and evaluate food service employees.
8. Conduct training sessions for new food service employees.
9. Inspect lunchroom and kitchen area daily to assure compliance with health, safety, and sanitation requirements.
10. Plan work schedules and coordinate daily work for efficient use of labor.
11. Maintain, prepare, and review a variety of menu production records, inventories, logs, and reports.
12. Perform other duties related to the position of food service manager.

Days of Employment

185 days/7.5 hours per day as per official school operational days as set by the Board of Education.

SALARY: Determined by the classified salary schedule of the school district.

JOB GRADING AND RELATED SALARY COMPENSATION

Not only does job analysis serve as the foundation for designing job descriptions for the many positions within the classified employees' world of work, but it also serves as the basis for *job grading* and the ultimate assignment of valuing compensation levels for the varying positions within each classified job family. Each classified job is assigned a *range figure* that is determined on the basis of the level of knowledge/skill, environmental factors, level of responsibility, level of supervision, human relations/contacts, level of education, depth of experience, and the immediate availability of qualified workers in the respective job categories.

Consider the criterion of required skill and knowledge for a specific job. A rating scale of 1 (low) to 4 (high) would be used to judge the nature of the position. The lowest rating of 1 would indicate that the job required little or no specialized knowledge or skill; a rating of 2 would indicate the job required specialized knowledge/skill common to all in the broad category under consideration; a rating of 3 would indicate that the job required a specialized level of knowledge/skill not common to all in the category being considered; and a rating of 4 would indicate that the job required a high level of knowledge/skill not common to all in the category being considered. Thus, a school custodian might be rated a 1 in the category of skill and knowledge and a registered electrician might be rated a 4.

Similarly, for the performance characteristic of the level of responsibility, a rating of 1 would mean that the person in the position was responsible for only the satisfactory performance the work which is assigned to him or her and is routine in nature. A rating of 2 would be given to an employee who was responsible for his or her own work but some work must be done independently and decided on personal initiative. A rating of 3 would be given for a position whereby the worker is responsible for the direction of an office/unit and has to make decisions which are in line with school district policy.

The highest job rating of 4 in the criterion of responsibility would be awarded to the employee who was responsible for a subdivision or division of the school system and was involved in decision making and policy development to aid that division in goal achievement.

CLASSIFIED SALARY SCHEDULES

The salary schedules of classified personnel contain three primary components: (1) the number years of experience in the job performed within the school district, (2) the payment levels, either hourly or annually, for each range level, and (3) the salary increases for each job grade level for years

Range	Years of Service							
	1	2	3	4	5–9	10–14	15–19	20
1	23,923.36	25,119.54	26,375.51	27,694.27	29,079.00	30,532.95	32,059.59	33,662.58
5	26,406.91	27,727.26	29,113.63	30,569.30	32,097.76	33,702.66	35,387.79	37,157.17
10	29,877.00	31,370.85	32,939.40	34,586.38	36,315.68	38,131.46	40,038.03	42,039.94
15	33,803.09	36,493.24	37,267.91	39,131.30	41,087.85	43,142.26	45,299.36	47,564.33
20	38,245.09	40,157.34	42,166.21	44,273.46	46,487.14	50,031.79	52,533.38	56,160.04
25	43,270.81	45,434.35	47,706.07	50,091.37	52,595.94	55,225.73	57,987.02	60,886.36
30	48,956.94	51,404.80	53,975.04	56,673.78	59,507.47	62,482.85	65,606.98	68,887.33
35	55,390.28	58,159.81	61,067.79	64,121.18	67,327.24	70,693.61	74,228.29	77,939.69
40	62,669.03	65,802.48	69,092.59	72,547.23	76,174.59	79,983.32	83,982.49	88,181.61

Figure 5.1. Classified Grade Levels and Compensation for Years of Experience (Selected Range Levels)

of experience. The Carlsbad Unified School District in Carlsbad, California, lists forty job range levels from lowest to highest. Figure 5.1 shows nine different job ranges with compensation payments for one to twenty years of service. As indicated, a classified employee at range level 10, with four years of service, would receive a salary of $34,586.38 for twelve months of work, eight hours per day.

Range 1, the lowest job level, would compensate a first-year employee a salary of $23,923.36. A worker in the highest range 40 would begin the first year at $62,669. In comparison, a certified first-year elementary school teacher currently has a beginning salary of approximately $33,706.

SUMMARY OF CLASSIFIED JOB FAMILIES

The most commonly named job families within classified personnel positions include (1) school office and clerical services, (2) school food services, (3) school maintenance and operations, (4) school transportation services, (5) para-educators and instructional assistants, and (6) special services for health, safety, security, and technological programming.

Each family of positions performs important work that supports the accomplishment of school goals and objectives. School office and clerical employees might be performing important communication and clerical work in the front office of a local school or providing administrative support in the school district's central office. Communication and service support requires special knowledge and skills in working with coworkers, school administrators, students, and parents.

School food services place classified personnel in school cafeterias and food preparation centers to provide food safety and nutrition for students. One might be surprised to learn that conflict management, communication skills, safety in the workplace, team building, listening skills, workplace courtesy, English and grammar, writing for results, leadership skills, time management, and other such skills are among the basic, advanced, and elective classes offered for classified personnel by the Kent School District of Kent, Washington. Professional growth and development activities are as important for classified personnel as they are for those individuals in certificated positions in our schools.

School maintenance and operations include work activities that serve to keep the school environment a safe and healthy place for employees to work and students to learn. The maintenance of school grounds and facilities is of vital importance. School transportation services center primarily on bus drivers who must transport students safely to and from the school on a daily basis. Although safety is first and foremost for personnel in this classified job family, the qualifications and work responsibilities of a school bus driver extend far beyond bus driving. The job description for a bus driver in one Arizona school system includes the following tasks that must be performed:

> Tasks: Transports students to and from school and on special events trips in a safe manner. Performs daily inspection of bus and prepares reports concerning maintenance needs; ensures bus is in good running condition by checking brakes, lights, and inside vehicle. Checks and monitors the conditions of the bus before and after the shift, ensures it is safe to operate; keeps bus clean inside and out; sweeps and mops floors, cleans windows to ensure good visibility. Inspects and maintains fluid levels; prepares repair orders, keeps written records and log sheets. Interacts with students, maintaining good student/driver relationships; maintains order and ensures safety and comfort of students; completes misconduct forms if necessary; performs other related duties as assigned.

CLASSIFIED EMPLOYEE TURNOVER

Employee turnover must not only consider the school district's turnover rate (number of separations during the fiscal year by the average number of classified employees during the fiscal year, then multiplied by 100), but must consider voluntary, involuntary, and in-district transfers as well. If a school district had 1,000 classified employees and 250 classified employees left the school district during the fiscal year, the turnover rate would be 25%.

However, turnover must consider voluntary separation, involuntary separation, and interschool district transfers as well. *Voluntary separation* is when the employee leaves the school district on his or her own accord. Retirement or leaving the school district for another position elsewhere is considered as voluntary separation. *Involuntary separation* is when the employee is dismissed by the district's school board, resignation in lieu of dismissal, reduction in force, death, and other causes whereby the employee's contract is not renewed.

Internal school or school unit transfer also affects a school's turnover rate even though the school district does not lose an employee. This occurs when a school teacher is promoted to a central office position in the school district's central office or a lead food service assistant is promoted to food service manager in another school within the school district. A local school is most interested in the statistic of total turnover since each loss necessitates the need for a replacement. Although the school district does not lose an employee, the local school does lose an important classified employee.

Although state reports on employee turnover are readily available, classified turnover statistics for local school districts are not. We asked several school principals about classified employee turnover rates and the most common responses were "turnover is ongoing" and "we train them and then they are hired by a community business or industry." Our best source for estimating classified employee turnover was the Texas Auditors Office and Louisiana Civil Service *Report on Turnover Rates for Non-Temporary Classified Employees* (State Civil Service, Louisiana, 2013–14). The turnover rate for classified employees in the state of Texas for 2015 was 18%. This turnover rate was an increase of 1.5% over the 16.8% in 2011. The three top reasons reported for leaving state employment during the fiscal year 2015 were for retirement, for better pay/benefits, and because of poor working conditions/environment.

The Louisiana Civil Service report included an interesting cost calculation for employee turnover.

The Mathis-Jackson model for costing turnover is as follows:

A = Typical annual pay for job
B = Percentage pay for benefits times ($\times$) annual pay
C.= Total employee annual cost (A + B)
D = Voluntary quits in the past twelve months
E = Time to become fully productive (in months)

F = Per person turnover cost: (multiply E divided by $12 \times C \times 50\%$) (Assumes 50% productivity throughout the learning period)

G = Annual turnover cost: $F \times D$

CERTIFICATED EMPLOYEE TURNOVER:
A RELATED STATISTIC

We have mentioned previously that teacher turnover ranges from 20% to 33% annually. Suppose a school district hired sixty new teachers at the beginning of the school year. At the end of their first year of teaching, 20% to 33% of that group would leave their positions in the district. After five years, approximately 50% of the group will have left the school district. So what? Won't the district simply hire new personnel to replace them? The results of certificated employee replacement are much more complicated.

Empirical evidence tells us that it costs 25% of a teacher's salary to replace the teacher. Thus, if a school district loses 20% of its certificated staff of 150 teachers making an average salary of $47,000, the cost of their replacement would be $352,500. The HR director does not have a magic wand to replace personnel; recruiting time, salary time, travel costs, and related administrative work are related replacement expenses. The loss of intellectual capital, training expense losses, loss of the knowledge base, and effects on organization stability loom important. The replacement cost of $352,500 is money that would be welcomed in other tight budgets facing the school district. The replacement of classified personnel involves similar cost factors.

Statistics reveal that 20% to 30% of the classified personnel are leaving the school district after the first year of service (Norton, 2008). Using the procedures set forth in the foregoing paragraph, assume that a school district employed seventy-five certificated personnel at an average salary of $29,000. We will assume that it costs 25% of the employee's salary to replace that employee. The loss of just 20% of the classified staff would cost the school district $108,750 to replace them. Administrative costs, employee training costs, experience loss, recruiting expenditures, and other employee replacement costs are factors of concern for classified personnel replacements as well.

The foregoing replacement costs are based on empirical evidence; we understand that such examples are not completely objective. The examples might serve to encourage human resources administrators to insert their school district's specific information into the cost procedures and compute a more realistic measure of replacement costs in their situations. For example, an informal study of replacement costs for the districts before and after specific program efforts for re-recruitment, work climate improvement, career promotion activities, and other employee relations efforts would provide hard data for review by school leaders and the school board and members of the school community.

RECRUITMENT STRATEGIES FOR CLASSIFIED PERSONNEL

Thus far in this chapter, we have identified the many job roles of classified workers in school systems nationally. In the following sections, we focus on recruiting, selecting, placing, orienting, evaluating, developing, and re-recruiting these important school workers. Previously, in chapter 2, we discussed the importance of planning and its components of forecasting, designing goals and objectives, strategizing procedures to reach the goals, organizing procedures, and gaining participation and cooperation in the process. With the planning process in place, the processes of re-recruiting, recruiting, selecting, and orienting both certificated and classified personnel can be implemented.

Human resources directors and school principals inform us that walk-ins constitute a large percentage of classified employee applications. Word spreads that the school district is a good place to work; salaries are competitive, fringe benefits are attractive, and chances for advancement on the job are positive. It is common for school principals to comment that present classified personnel are among the very best job recruiters. Other recruitment sources include employment services, departments of economic security, newspaper ads, and other electronic job listing services. It is common to see position opening announcements for classified personnel at movie theaters and through periodic job fairs.

As mentioned previously in this chapter, the hiring process for classified personnel tends to parallel the process for certificated personnel. The following school board policy for the Orange County School Board exemplifies the purposes common to most school districts nationally. However, the following school district policy tends to include the ingredients of an administrative regulation in that it tends to set forth specific administrative procedures to be followed. Effective *school policies* serve to establish the goals and objectives of the personnel function and the aims that the policy is to achieve. It answers the question of "What to do?" An *administrative regulation* is specific in its statements regarding how the policy is to be achieved.

Classified Personnel Policy

Policy Number 7207
Reviewed and Approved by the Board of Education
Employment of classified personnel shall be on the recommendation of an associate superintendent and the supervisor and principals who will

supervise the work of such employees. All letters of application and other pertinent information concerning prospective classified personnel available for employment should be received by these administrators.

After the applicant's information has been processed and approved as eligible for employment, the administrator in need of such personnel is to invite the applicant to have a personal interview.

The administrator may not make any commitment to the prospective employee for a position in the district. If the administrator wishes to recommend the prospect for the position(s), he is to make a recommendation to the Associate Superintendent or designee.

Classified personnel shall be hired only upon the approval of the Superintendent and Board of Education.

All candidates shall be considered on the needs of the district and on the basis of their merits and qualifications. There shall be no discrimination or preferential treatment with regard to race, national origin, gender, creed, color, sexual orientation, or age in the selection process. In each instance, the Superintendent and others involved in the selection process shall seek to employ the best qualified person for the position.

THE JOB APPLICATION

An effective job application for a classified employee position should include sufficient information that can be used to determine if the applicant should be placed in the official applicant pool, although it should not be so lengthy as to discourage a prospective employee from applying for a position. The following job application form gives full consideration to several primary informational components: (1) personal information including full name, address, work authorization, citizenship, home phone, and availability; (2) personal data, including driving license and job licensing; (3) work experience with position(s) held and time allocations; (4) formal education history; (5) special training, including workshops, trade schools, business schools, and others; (6) personal references, including previous work supervisors' names, positions, contacts; and (7) approval to conduct a background check if prescribed. The following is an example of an application for a classified employee position.

ETNOM SCHOOL DISTRICT

Classified Employee Application Form

Personal Information

Name: _____   Date: _____

Current Address: _____

Phone: _____   Email Address: _____

Work area or position of application:_____

Current Employment (List position and location of work): _____

_____

In reference to your employment interests/qualifications, answer each of the following:

1. How has your previous work experience and/or training prepared you for the position that you are interested in or applying for?
2. Describe the specific knowledge and skills that you possess that would serve in a positive way in a position in the Etnom School District.
3. Explain how you used your current knowledge and skills to personally resolve a work site problem or meet a program objective in your previous work experience.
4. List the names, positions, and addresses of at least three persons who have supervised your work previously or know your work experience especially well.

Other information that you view as relevant to the purposes of this employment application:

_____

_____

_____

CLASSIFIED EMPLOYEE RECRUITMENT POOL

It has become increasingly important to process classified applications expeditiously. The availability factor for applicants with certain knowledge and skills conditions and establishes the need for immediate follow-up. If the application form gives evidence of a highly qualified applicant for a position that has experienced a limited number of applicants, an immediate telephone interview is advisable. *Application screening* involves an objective procedure for ranking and determining those applicants who will be placed in the applicant pool. A follow-up communication by e-mail or a five-minute telephone call is important for informing each applicant who has been placed in the applicant pool. One or two questions are appropriate at this time: "What is the status of your interest for the position(s) in question at this time?" and

"What about your availability for an interview either by telephone or in person within a reasonable period of time?"

The school district representative has the opportunity to meet the applicant and to show a positive interest in his or her application. The caller also will learn more about the applicant's interest in participating in follow-up activities of the selection process. Oral communication, enthusiasm, courtesy, and other affective characteristics held by the applicant might be observed in the brief telephone call as well. At the time of the call and with positive results, the school district representative would be wise to schedule a follow-up personal interview with the applicant. Keep in mind, especially if the school district is using recruitment services by employment services on the Web, that many other school districts are likely to be competing for the same applicants.

Personal interviews for classified applicants vary. In some cases, performance tests, simulation exercises, and other evaluation activities are implemented. A written exam might be administered to test the specific knowledge of a candidate for a position requiring specialized technical knowledge. A test of performance provides an opportunity for the candidate to show his or her actual skill in relation to a task required in the job. A simulation exercise places the candidate in a situation that the person is likely to face while on the job; the candidate takes the place of a person on the job and reacts as he or she would if actually on the job.

Applicants for the position of a school secretary, security guard, social worker, parent liaison worker, parent aide, or other such positions that require communication and relationship skills might be asked to participate in a real-life situation relative to the position at hand. Affective characteristics such as judgment, courtesy, listening, enthusiasm, communication, and fairness are likely to be observed through the use of these simulation strategies.

NOMINATING CANDIDATES FOR HIRING

Three basic principles are to be followed in hiring personnel for positions in public schools: (1) The school superintendent receives recommendations for hire from the human resources director, appropriate school principal, or other authorized school official. (2) The school superintendent, in turn, presents the final listing of recommended hires to the school board at an official meeting of the board. (3) The school board acts on the final approval of the recommended hires.

However, legally, the hiring is not official until a contract has been signed by the new employee and the results of the required background check have been examined and assessed. Of course, letters of acceptance of hire are sent to each person newly hired with the information often required by the state, such as authority to work in the United States, immunization requirements, fingerprinting, and results of the required background check.

An important final step in the hiring process is the assessment and evaluation of the selection process. How effective were the plans and procedures for the recruitment and selection processes? Accountability measures for determining the effectiveness of recruitment in terms of numbers and costs were discussed previously in the chapter. A follow-up assessment of the retention of those employees hired should be addressed after the first year of service.

Suppose sixty-five classified employees were hired last year and of that group forty-two remained for the second year of service. The retention rate is 69% or a turnover of 31%. What needs to be done in our recruitment, selection, and orientation processes to reduce the turnover rate in the future? How effective was our re-recruitment efforts?

THE VITAL IMPORTANCE OF THE CLASSIFIED EMPLOYEE TRAINING PROCESS

How much do you know about growth and development programs for classified personnel in your school district? Previously in this chapter, we listed ten specific classes in the training program for food and nutrition employees. The development classes ranged from conflict management to team building, to leadership skills, to listening skills, and other affective and cognitive skills. What development classes might come to your mind for classified workers in the job family of business/accounting or para-educator?

Previous discussions of the orientation process for certificated personnel apply to classified workers as well. *Pre-employment orientation* is those activities generally provided during the period between initial contact with the school district and the time the individual assumes an assignment in the school district. *Post-employment orientation* is implemented following employment and focuses on providing for the effective and efficient transition of personnel into specific position roles. Employee orientation is inextricably tied to the staff development process.

Effective orientation programs serve several primary growth and development purposes by (1) facilitating an effective transition of new classified personnel into the school district and specific job to which they are assigned, (2) underscoring the importance of understanding and committing to the mission and vision of the school and school district, (3) reducing or removing problems that inhibit work effectiveness, (4) identifying the special talents of workers that can be utilized more efficiently to achieve the purposes of the position at hand. According to Peter Drucker (2004), effective executives put their best people on opportunities rather than on problems, (5) increasing the job satisfaction of the employee through the implication of effective supervisory support and (6) giving assurance to the employee that his or her job responsibilities are of special importance to the overall achievement of the school district's goals and objectives.

ACCOUNTABILITY MEASURES FOR EMPLOYEE DEVELOPMENT ACTIVITIES

It would be difficult to find a school district nationally that did not have some program for classified employee improvement. Commonly, improvement activities are offered for every job family in oral and written communication, workplace courtesy, conflict management, and other affective characteristics. Employment reports tend to report the development results in terms of the number of employees who completed the program activity or program evaluation results that a high percentage of the participants enjoyed the experience. What is missing are hard data that focus on the actual results of positive outcomes for improved practices.

Hard data questions are more appropriate. That is, were the program activities job embedded? If so, what specific outcomes were in evidence from the implementation of the knowledge and skills gained in the improvement activity? Did the improvement program result in a higher job classification for some workers in a job family as a result of the completion of a specified development program and the successful passing of testing results? Which of the following data are of highest accountability? How many classified employees attended the safety in the workplace program? A typical answer would be as follows: accidents related to the work of classified employees were reduced by 25% in the six-month period following a program they attended on safety in the workplace.

Effective classified improvement activities must find their accountability in the manner in which they benefit the worker, the school, and the school district in which they are employed. It's a two-way street: the school district supports the improvement interests and needs of each individual classified employee so that he or she can, in turn, give an improved support to the stated mission and vision of the school and school district.

CLASSIFIED EMPLOYEE PERFORMANCE EVALUATION

Performance evaluation for classified personnel is both formative and summative. A *formative evaluation* is based on the purposes related to the improvement of performance. It has become more common for the local school principal to serve as the evaluator for classified personnel working within the principal's local school.

A cooperative employee evaluation strategy is demonstrated by one implemented by the Eugene, Oregon School District. The process is initiated by the use of a self-evaluation by the employee. Figure 5.2 sets forth the self-evaluation form that is completed by the classified employee and sent to the employee's local supervisor. The local supervisor reviews the self-evaluation and follows the review by scheduling a discussion with the worker to discuss

Classified Employee Self-Assessment

Date: _____

Employee Name:_____ Employee
Number_____

Location Department:_____ Position
Title:_____

Directions: Please rate yourself on each indicator and send the form to your supervisor. Attach additional comment sheets if necessary.

	Ineffective	Area for Growth	Effective	Exemplary
1. Quality of Work	[ ]	[ ]	[ ]	[ ]
2. Quantity of Work	[ ]	[ ]	[ ]	[ ]
3. Job Knowledge	[ ]	[ ]	[ ]	[ ]
4. Job Skills	[ ]	[ ]	[ ]	[ ]
5. Flexibility/Adaptability	[ ]	[ ]	[ ]	[ ]
6. Initiative	[ ]	[ ]	[ ]	[ ]
7. Judgment/Decision	[ ]	[ ]	[ ]	[ ]
8. Organization	[ ]	[ ]	[ ]	[ ]
9. Efficiency	[ ]	[ ]	[ ]	[ ]
10. Equipment Maintenance	[ ]	[ ]	[ ]	[ ]
11. Safety	[ ]	[ ]	[ ]	[ ]
12. Compliance w/Policies	[ ]	[ ]	[ ]	[ ]
13. Attendance	[ ]	[ ]	[ ]	[ ]
14. Punctuality	[ ]	[ ]	[ ]	[ ]
15. Relationships w. Others	[ ]	[ ]	[ ]	[ ]

A. What do you see as your accomplishments during the evaluation period and your major strengths?

B. Considering the areas where growth may be needed, what goal(s) will you consider for the next evaluation period?

C. What might your supervisor do or provide to support and assist you in the next evaluation period?

Signature

Name of Employee

(printed)_____

Employee's
Signature_____

Figure 5.2.   Classified Employee Self-Assessment Form

Source: Eugene, Oregon School District. Classified Employee Self-Assessment. Human Resources, April 2016.

the employee's work and employment expectations. Note that the fifteen performance indicators are briefly described in the actual self-evaluation form. For example, the indicator of Quality of Work states that work is accurate, thorough, neat, and completed in a timely manner.

PROFESSIONAL DEVELOPMENT GUIDELINES

The Mesa Public Schools of Mesa, Arizona, sets forth a comprehensive statement of professional development guidelines for classified personnel. Eligibility requirements include the following: how the professional development credits are earned, how the professional development credits are calculated, how the professional development credits can be counted toward additional compensation, and how the classified classes are approved.

A classified professional development committee oversees the professional development activities; the executive director of human resources and human resources supervisor serve on the committee along with other school representatives. The school district's unique form for requesting approval of professional development credit is shown in Figure 5.3.

Classified Employees

Employee Name_____
Date:_____

Job Title:_____   Work
Site_____

Title of Course, Workshop or Program
Activity;_____

Institution or Activity
Source:_____

Professional Development Credits to be
Earned:_____

Describe how the professional development activity is relevant to your
position/job_____

_____

Describe how the professional development activity will be beneficial to the school/school
district_____

_____

Submit to the HR Director of Human Resources   To be completed by Human Resources
Committee:

Committee Review Date_____

Approval _____Yes   _____No

Confirmation sent to employee—
Date_____

Figure 5.3.   Request for Approval of Professional Development Credit

EMPLOYEE ASSISTANCE PROGRAMS: WHY AND WHAT FOR?

Human resources leaders have recognized that unsolved problems of classified personnel will have an adverse effect on the employee's performance.
Employment Assistance Programs serve employees in positive ways: keeping
the school alert to and helping the school identify the problematic concerns
of employees, providing assistance to the worker in finding solutions and
needed treatment, giving guidance for appropriate providers that can best
counsel and direct the worker in relation to the problem, and protect the personal worth and dignity of the troubled employee.

The former singular focus on alcohol problems of employees has expanded
to consider all behavioral and personal problems of the employee. Chemical
dependency, family and marital problems, legal matters, financial concerns,
and health problems are such examples. Some problems of the employee can
be resolved by services provided within the school district, such as personal
counseling, financial counseling, referral services, and health promotion
programs.

The human resources unit of the school district should establish procedures for ascertaining signs of personal problems demonstrated by the
employee's behavioral signals and work effectiveness, being knowledgeable
of assistance programs that are available for troubled personnel, implementing effective personnel counseling services, and paying close attention to
matters related to the worker's position assignment, such as workload, environment, special measures relating to open communication, and mentoring
services. Management Mentors (2016) points out that "retention affects the
bottom line not only by reducing costs, but also by building an effective
workforce" (p. 5).

CLASSIFIED PERSONNEL: SUSPENSION AND DISMISSAL

State statutes commonly set forth procedures for the suspension and dismissal
of classified personnel. State requirements are then reflected in suspension
and policy statements by the local school board. Court rulings have made it
clear that classified personnel do not have the expectation of long-term property rights such as those for the tenure for certificated personnel. Nevertheless, classified personnel do have certain rights under the First Amendment to
the United States Constitution and instances when illegal discrimination can
be established by the classified employee.

The following excerpt from a school board policy of the Pitt County Board
of Education of Greenville, NC (2015) is an example that includes many

provisions common to board policies nationally. Note that only the entire suspension policy is set forth in the following section. The opening statement in the school board's dismissal policy is included in the following example but the follow-up procedures are not. Follow-up procedures for the dismissal policy are quite similar to those set forth in the suspension section of the example.

Classified Personnel: Suspension and Dismissal

Classified positions are critical to the effective operation of the school system . . . All employees are expected to meet job requirements and to seek clarification and guidance when needed to fulfill these requirements.

A. Suspension

The superintendent or designee may suspend an employee without pay as a disciplinary sanction. The superintendent shall provide written notice of the suspension without pay to the employee . . . The suspension without pay may begin immediately. An employee has 10 calendar days from the date of receiving written notice of the superintendent's suspension to take the following actions: (1) request written notice of the reason(s) for the superintendent's decision and (2) request an appeal before the board of education regarding the decision to suspend without pay. If notice for the reason(s) for the suspension is requested, such notice shall be provided prior to any board hearing on the decision. If an appeal is not made within this time, an appeal is deemed to be waived.

An employee may appeal a suspension on the grounds that there was not rational basis for the suspension; the suspension was discriminatory or was used for harassment; or board policies were not followed.

Upon receiving a request for an appeal, the chairperson may designate a panel of three board members to review the decision. The chairperson of the board or the panel may establish rules for an orderly and efficient hearing. The employee will be notified in writing of the decision of the board to uphold, reverse, or modify the superintendent's decision. An employee will receive back pay for any period of suspension without pay that is not upheld by the board.

B. Termination

As "at will" employees, employees in classified positions may be terminated on any nondiscriminatory basis, including inadequate performance, misconduct, failure to follow board policies, or a reduction in staff. All terminations to reduce staff will be accordance with policy 7211, Classified Personnel Reduction in Force. All other terminations will be made pursuant to this policy. The superintendent should provide written notice to the employee and the board of the decision to terminate.

Table 5.1. Reasons for Employee Turnover

Reason for Leaving the Position	Average Point Rating
Pay and Benefits	2.8
Work Conditions, Workload, or Work Schedule	2.7
Agency Policies or Practices	2.4
Immediate Supervisor or Coworkers	2.4
Need for More Challenging and Meaningful Work	2.1

The State of Texas completed a comprehensive report entitled *Classified Employee Turnover for Fiscal Year 2015.* One topic of the report centered on the specific reasons that influenced an employee's decision to leave employment with his or her agency. The following results were calculated from the state's exit survey. The average number of responses for each of the five *influences* was 3,629 employees. It is important to keep in mind that the participants in the exit interviews resigned voluntarily from their state positions. Ratings for each of the five basic reasons for leaving their positions were computed on a 5-point scale: 1, very little extent; 2, little extent; 3, some extent; 4, great extent; 5, very great extent. The five specific influences on decisions to leave along with their average point rating are shown in Table 5.1.

As is shown in the decision results, the average influences ranged from 2.1 (very close to little extent) to 2.8 (close to some extent). Nevertheless, the two leading reasons for leaving their state positions centered on pay and benefits and work conditions, workload, or work schedule. We have not found a similar exit study for classified personnel in K-12 school settings. Such a statewide study would, in our opinion, be of special interest and value.

Take a few minutes to complete the following post-quiz related to growth and development training for other classified personnel. If you do especially well on the quiz, perhaps you can skip the rest of this chapter. However, don't just guess the answer; rather, just skip that question and move on to the next one.

POST-QUIZ

1. Which of the following performance responsibilities are commonly listed in the job description of a food service manager? Circle each entry that would apply.
   a. Shall communicate effectively both orally and in writing with parents, students, and faculty.

   b. Shall have demonstrated people skills to indicate the ability to function in a team-oriented environment.

   c. Shall have the ability to sit, stoop, possibly lift up to 50 pounds or more.

   d. Shall strive to maintain and improve professional competence.

   e. Shall complete a training course for certification of beginning school food service personnel as prescribed in state statutes.

2. Performance management centers on which of the following processes?
   a. The act of appraising or evaluating the performance of individual employees.
   b. Determining to what extent an employee or job family has performed in relation to stated goals and objectives.
   c. The activities, processes, services, or programs that the school leaders create to manage the performance of employees or job families within the school district.
   d. A method used to assess the employee's qualifications for a specific position of employment.
   e. None of the above.

3. Development and training experiences for classified employees should be
   a. job embedded.
   b. waived when the basic knowledge and skills of the job can be demonstrated by the employee.
   c. most effective when determined by the human resources director for classified personnel since he or she is best informed as to the school district's needs.
   d. designed for the primary purpose of remediating weaknesses of individual employees.
   e. unnecessary for classified employees when a job description has been developed for the position in question.

4. A formative evaluation for a classified employee of the school district is
   a. associated with making decisions about job continuation, grade level placement with a job family, and defining worker compensation levels.
   b. a procedure that takes place during the hiring that proves to determine if the candidate has the qualities to be considered for employment in the school system.
   c. a process for determining the focus of the employee's individual development plan.
   d. an evaluation that has goals that center on professional development and improvement.

5. The administration of performance evaluation procedures for classified employees has
    a. decreased in "popularity" since position descriptions set forth the requirements for a specific position and individuals are hired according to their qualifications for meeting the requirements set forth.
    b. been dropped by school districts nationally due to the increasing difficulty of hiring and retaining classified personnel.
    c. never been more popular and has received more attention in the popular press than in recent times.
    d. been dropped by the majority of school districts nationally since classified employee retention has been "impossible" to control and its productive outcomes have shown negative results on employee improvement.

6. Professional development guidelines for classified personnel, for the most part, are
    a. missing from the policies and administrative regulations of school districts.
    b. readily available for reference and use by classified employees of school districts.
    c. determined exclusively by one person in the school district, such as the director of human resources, supervisor of classified personnel, or the local school principal.
    d. self-development improvement options that the individual worker plans and utilizes.

7. NSDTA stands for
    a. National Staff Development and Training Association.
    b. a model for a classified evaluation process (*N*eeds, *S*tandards, *D*evelopment, *T*echniques, and *A*ssessments).
    c. necessary standards, determinants, tests for achievement (for classified personnel).
    d. National School Department for Technological Advancement.

8. The terms *classified personnel, support personnel, staff personnel*, and *non-certificated personnel* are
    a. commonly viewed as synonymous.
    b. commonly used to separate the differences between job families.
    c. commonly used as separate terms to identify business/accounting personnel, maintenance/facilities personnel, clerical/secretarial personnel, and central office workers in that order.

9. From a legal standpoint, an employee's position description is viewed as
   a. part of his or her employment contract.
   b. an unofficial guide for helping the worker decide what priorities should be considered for his or her workday.
   c. a means of controlling the work activities of the employee.
   d. a means for freezing the responsibilities of the worker in place.

10. A school secretary
    a. does not have a reasonable expectation of permanent employment and thus is not entitled to a due process hearing on dismissal.
    b. has the same rights as a certificated teacher regarding permanent employment.

11. A female custodian on the same grade level and years of experience as a male custodian must be paid the same salary as a male custodian. ____True or ____False

12. Discharge and/or refusal to employ applicants as teacher aides because they are unwed has been ruled by the courts as permissible. ___True or ____False

13. A classified employee's personnel rights closely parallel those of certificated personnel. ____True or ____False

14. Human resources practices for classified personnel parallel those for certificated personnel in many ways. ____True or ____False

15. Job grading for classified personnel is synonymous with position analysis for certificated personnel. ____True or ____False

16. A classified employee in a school district holds a grade range of 20 and has fifteen years of experience with the school district. Using the salary schedule for classified personnel set forth in Figure 5.1, what is his annual salary?
    a. $42,039.94
    b. $47,564.33
    c. $52,333.38
    d. Cannot be calculated by using Figure 5.1

Answers to the Post-Quiz

The answer to question 1 is a, b, c, d, and e; answer to question 2 is c; answer to question 3 is a; answer to question 4 is d; answer to question 5 is c; answer to question 6 is b; answer to question 7 is a; answer to question 8 is a; answer to question 9 is a; answer to question 10 is a; question 11 is true; question 12 is false; question 13 is true; question 14 is true; question 15 is false; answer to question 16 is c.

Discussion of the Post-Quiz

1. All of the responses for question 1 are common entries in the job responsibilities of food service managers. Effective characteristics such as communication and people skills are included in virtually every job description of a classified employee. In fact, classified employee performance assessment forms typically include such characteristics as interpersonal relations, communication skills, team building, and other affective characteristics. The point to be underscored here is that although technical skills are important for classified employees, affective skills loom important for effectiveness as well. The general work characteristics of dependability, interpersonal relations, team building, and attendance/punctuality loom important in all positions with the many classified job families.

2. *Performance management* includes the activities, processes, or programs that school leaders create to manage the employment of employees or job families within the school district. Sometimes, it is helpful to define a term such as *performance management* by stating what it is not. Performance management is not an evaluation/appraisal session whereby the performance of an employee is assessed. Performance management is not an assessment tool or strategy whereby the employee completes a self-evaluation. Performance management does include a number of human resources processes, including employee orientation activities, establishing competency-based performance expectations, determination of ongoing individual development plans, and opportunities for career recognition and advancement. In short, Heathfield (2016) states that "performance management is a process of creating a work environment or setting in which people are enabled to perform to the best of their abilities" (p. 1).

3. Development and training experiences for classified employees are job embedded. This means that, to be effective, classified employee growth activities must be meaningful and applicable to the improvement of their work responsibilities; training activities must focus on the personal interests and needs of the individual worker as they enhance his or her ability to be more successful in meeting the responsibilities of the job. Lunenburg and Ornstein (2004) recommend that a *needs analysis* precede the planning and implementation of a training program; the needs of the entire school system, needs of the special group of workers in the job family, and needs of the specific individuals in the job family serve as the focus for the needs analysis.

   A successful staff development program is (1) relevant and reflects the current projected needs of the staff and the school district, (2) developmental in that it is concerned with upward growth rather than remedial training, (3) multifaceted in that it incorporates a variety of activities and strategies, (4) founded on the needs and assessments of the particular roles of job family groups and individuals, and (5) based on the concept that the school system will progress as the individuals within the job families grow and develop.

As noted previously in the book, the strategies of adult learning must be kept in mind. How do adults learn best? What is the most effective learning style for the individual worker? How best can the employee become engaged in the learning/improvement process?

4. A *summative evaluation* for a classified employee of the school district is associated with making decisions about job continuation, grade level placement with a job family, and defining worker compensation levels. Such an evaluation tends to raise the question as to who should be doing the *formative evaluation*, which centers on determining job continuation, promotion, or other meritorious purposes. The problem centers on whether a school principal, for example, can work effectively with the employee relative to the positive relationships needed in a cooperative improvement process and then be the one to evaluate the individual for retention purposes.

One might contend that the foregoing procedure is common to current practice. Yet, if the employee is aware that the person working with him or her on improvement is the one who ultimately will decide the question of retention, divulging present needs or asking for help in regard to one's weaknesses is problematic. We support the plan whereby one administrator works with the employee on formative evaluations. Then, another qualified school leader administers the necessary summative evaluation/assessment results.

5. The administration of performance evaluation procedures for classified employees has never been more popular and has received more attention in the popular press in recent times. Part of the reason is vested in the realization that classified personnel have important roles to play in the achievement of school district goals and objectives. An examination of any one of the many position descriptions of classified personnel not only reveals the requirement for special knowledge and skills but also sets forth specific affective requirements for effectiveness on the job. For example, the classified job description of a budget director for the Boyd County Public Schools of Ashland, Kentucky, lists the following entries among the general duties and performance responsibilities: (1) Shall present a positive image of the school to parents, and convey to them the school's genuine concern for education, growth, and development of each student, (2) shall seek to establish friendly and cooperative partnerships between home and school, and (3) shall work to develop a positive public relationship between the school district and the community.

The evaluation and assessment of classified employee performance serve as the basis for individual performance improvement, setting the employee's individual career objectives, and determining the employee's progress for career advancement. An effective performance evaluation can serve to recognize the strengths of the individual worker, reinforcing the appropriate performance behaviors related to the job responsibilities and fostering the factors of self-esteem, job satisfaction, cooperative relationships, and productivity of the classified employee.

6. Professional development guidelines for classified personnel, for the most part, are readily available for reference and use by classified employees of school districts. An examination of the policies, administrative regulations, employee handbooks, and orientation activities of school districts nationally will find professional growth and development for classified personnel among the school district's major program activities. The detailed program availability for personal growth in school district publications often tends to surpass the activities set forth for certificated personnel. One reason for this occurrence is that professional development for classified personnel most often is tied to upgrades in work positions within the job family.

7. NSDTA, or the National Staff Development and Training Association, is an affiliate of the American Public Human Services Association. Its stated mission is to build professional and organizational capacity in the human services through a national network of membership sharing ideas and resources on organizational development, staff development, and training. Its conferences have focused on learning activities that could be used in both training and educational settings. Emphasis is placed on training that is specific to human service issues.

8. The terms *classified personnel, support personnel, staff personnel,* and *non-certificated personnel* are synonymous. Although the title *classified personnel* is the most commonly used term, each of the foregoing terms refer to employees who do not require state certification. Some classified personnel positions do require licenses or have certain other training/experiences; they may not be certified by state statute.

9. From a legal standpoint, an employee's position description is viewed as part of his or her employment contract. Court cases have supported this contention historically. For example, if a custodian's job description specifically lists duty hours from 8:00 a.m. to 4:00 p.m. each weekday, he or she cannot be required to work a night shift from 4:00 p.m. to 12:00 p.m. The custodian can change work schedules if the agreement is reached to do so.

10. A school secretary does not have reasonable expectations of permanent employment and thus is not entitled to a due process hearing on

dismissal. The answer (a) is true but does depend on certain exceptions, such as when the employee claims that discriminatory factors were used in the dismissal or that statements made in the dismissal charges were such that would endanger the employee's future career opportunities or based on a violation of the employee's constitutional rights. The proof of a right's violation is placed on the employee. First Amendment rights are enjoyed by both certificated and classified personnel.

11. The statement that a female custodian on the same grade level and with the same years of experience as a male custodian must be paid the same as a male custodian is true. The Equal Pay Act states that jobs need not be identical, but they must be substantially equal. Job content, not titles, determine whether jobs are substantially equal.

12. The statement "Discharge and/or refusal to employ applicants as teacher aides because they are unwed has been ruled by the courts as permissible" is false. Courts have ruled such action as discriminatory.

13. A classified employee's personnel rights closely parallel those of certificated personnel, although there are important differences between certificated teacher rights and those of classified personnel. However, differences are not related to the rights given to every American citizen by the First Amendment of the United States Constitution ("Congress shall make no law respecting an establishment of religion, or prohibiting the exercise thereof, or abridging the freedom of speech, or of the press, or the right of the people to assemble, and to petition the government for a redress of grievances"). However, state statutes and school board policies do differ for certificated and classified personnel in terms of such provisions as non-renewal and dismissal. In any case, "When an employee is dismissed, evidence of the employee's prior misconduct is admissible" (*Daggs v. Boonville School District*, 508, w.W.l2nd 46, Ark. 1974).

14. The statement "Human resources practices for classified personnel parallel those for certificated personnel in many ways" is true. We have underscored the truth of this statement on several occasions throughout this chapter. The processes of recruitment, selection, assignment, orientation, development, and evaluation are common to HR practices related to both types of employees. Training methods for classified personnel do differ in many ways from those for certificated personnel, but strategies for recruiting and re-recruiting, selection, and other HR processes follow similar procedural models.

15. *Job grading* for classified personnel is based on the determination of job: preparation, knowledge and skills, position responsibilities, years of experience, supervisory responsibilities, and other factors such as the availability of personnel for the position(s) in question. *Position analysis*

is a scientific activity that centers on describing a position in detail relative to both internal and external factors that determine the job's environment. A position analysis includes the direct participation of the worker(s) with a follow-up assessment of the *position analysis* by the worker's supervisor. Similarities and differences in the opinions about the responsibilities, skills, knowledge, and inhibiting factors of the work environment are discussed and *resolved* through the cooperative actions of the worker(s) and supervisor(s).

16. The grade range of 20 on the salary scale has an annual salary of $52,533.38 for a worker with fifteen to nineteen years of experience.

THE LEGAL RIGHTS OF CLASSIFIED PERSONNEL

Classified personnel have the same rights as any other citizen of the United States. However, the totality of their legal rights is based primarily on the statutes set forth by the legislature of state in which the individual is employed. It would be safe to say that the large majority of rights of classified employees in the fifty states are similar. That is, classified employee rights commonly include provisions for certain fringe benefits, sick leave, overtime pay, leaves, collective bargaining, healthful workplace, protection from discrimination and sexual harassment, and so forth. In addition, the results of collective bargaining might bring about rights and provisions that are the same, similar or different among the various states.

It is beyond the scope of this chapter to give a comprehensive discussion of the legal world of the classified employee. We recommend the book *The Legal World of the School Principal: What Leaders Need to Know about School Law* (Norton, 2016) for human resources directors, school assistant principals and principals, teachers, classified personnel, and other school leaders for guidance relative to school law. However, the following listing sets forth the most common rights/provisions that are provided for classified employees in K-12 schools nationally. Note that the following rights listing is based on the document *Know Your Rights*, publication 311 of the California School Employees Association, San Jose, California (October 2009).

Title of Classified Employee Right or Provision with Definition

Personnel Files—Employees have the right to review their personnel file and enter into their file responses to negative documents.
Compensation/Wages—Earned compensation/wages are the property of the employee.
Overtime Pay—Employees have the right to overtime pay.

Benefits—Classified employees are entitled to benefits relating to vacation, holidays, sick leave, industrial accident and illness, bereavement leave, pregnancy and/or family leave, personal leave, jury duty, military leave.

Hours of Employment—Employees' workweek and workday must be set.

Collective Bargaining Rights—Employees have the right to negotiate.

Safety Devices—Employees must be provided with safety devices.

Safety, Healthful Workplace—Employees are entitled to a safe and healthful workplace.

Safety, Unsafe Workplace—Employees have the right to refuse to perform unsafe work.

Layoff and Reemployment—Employees have the right to notice, seniority, displacement, reemployment, and retirement.

Discipline and Due Process—Employees have the right to due process, including the right to receive written notice of charges, the right to be represented, and the right to informal and informal responses.

Sexual Harassment—Employees cannot be sexually harassed (Title VII of the Civil Rights Act Of 1964).

Discrimination and Harassment—Classified employees cannot be denied employment/advancement for discriminatory reasons.

Unemployment Compensation Insurance—Employees may be entitled to unemployment compensation when they are involuntarily employed.

Family and Medical Leave Act—Employees are entitled to leave under the Family and Medical Leave Act (FMLA).

Key Chapter Ideas and Recommendations

- The strategic importance of the classified employees of a school district tends to be overlooked in school districts. Yet, the complexity of the many job families within the classified employee personnel deserves the special attention of the human resources unit and local school principals within the school district due to the significant roles these employees play toward the accomplishment of the vision and mission of the school system.
- The human resources processes of recruiting, re-recruiting, selection, orientation, development, and others are common to those HR processes in place for certificated personnel. Effective administrative practices such as planning, organization, implementation, and evaluation must be exercised for classified employees, as is done in the case of effective practices for certificated personnel.
- Job analyses and job descriptions are of primary importance for the classified personnel function. The nature of job families within the classified personnel function, the necessity of job grading, compensation administration, employee evaluation, and career advancement are inextricably tied

to effective procedures of job analysis and the resulting designing of job descriptions.

- The problem of classified employee turnover takes its toll on the stability and effectiveness of efforts to meet program responsibilities, goals, and objectives. Much more attention must be given to this problem in the recruitment, selection, orientation, and re-recruitment of classified employees. Turnover cost factors are most important. The ways to determine turnover costs, as set forth in the chapter, must be studied in programs of preparation for HR administrators.

- School boards must examine and assess their classified employee policies annually. In addition, the human resources unit of the school district, school superintendent, and local school principals must also examine and assess the administrative regulations that center on classified personnel procedures. Each major human resource process (e.g., recruitment, selection, orientation, evaluation) should be updated/revised to meet the ever-changing issues and problems facing the human resources function in school districts.

- Local school principals increasingly have been delegated responsibilities for administering/supervising the classified personnel within their school sites. Preparation institutions for school administrators must give far more attention to the administration of the classified personnel function. Special development programs for school principals on the topic of classified personnel administration must be planned and implemented in school districts nationally as well.

- Professional development programs for classified personnel must be continued and improved and must be job embedded, tied to career upgrading, and given compensatory rewards.

DISCUSSION QUESTIONS

1. The final topic of this chapter centered on the troubled worker. To what extent do you believe your school district and its human resources leaders are giving effective attention to helping the troubled employee? In what ways do you see the needed services for troubled employees in operation? What recommendations might you have for improving this service?

2. This chapter reiterated the importance of job analyses and job descriptions for classified personnel. Review the section in the chapter that discusses these processes and set forth in writing how these processes are important in the administration of the classified personnel function.

3. Turnover of classified employees has been calculated to average from 20% to 30% annually. Assume that you have been asked to set forth a recommendation to the school board regarding strategies for reducing the turnover rate of classified employees. List several recommendations that will be included in your report to the school board.

4. Take time to reexamine the position of the food service manager set forth toward the beginning of this chapter. Develop a preparation program of fifteen hours that you believe would be appropriate for a person who aspires to the manager's position. What classes, on-hand experiences, and other learning activities would be appropriate in such a preparation program?

5. Regardless of your present position or work experience in the area of human resources administration, what information, topic, strategy, or general content was most interesting or perhaps new to you? How might an idea relative to your findings be implemented in your current work responsibilities?

6. Review the compensation in Figure 5.1. Explain the compensation procedures illustrated and how the classified salary schedule is similar or different from a single salary schedule for certificated personnel.

7. Salary schedules for classified personnel commonly are based on hourly pay or an annual salary for regular employees who work nine to twelve months a year. Explain why many schedules are based on hourly pay.

8. Classified employee development and performance evaluation were emphasized in this chapter. In regard to the several job families found in school districts today, set forth several ways in which employee accountability is implemented in the work of classified personnel.

9. The supervision of classified personnel has increasingly been delegated to local school principals. What are the implications of this supervisory role for school principals in terms of requirements for new knowledge and skills, course work during training and preparation for school administration, and legal matters that the principal will inevitably encounter?

10. Consider the program activities in relation to troubled employees. To what extent is the human resources unit of your school or a school in which you are most familiar providing needed services for troubled workers? Is there evidence available that indicates the school district rates a score of "highly satisfactory" in regard to its employee assistance program? Why or why not?

CASE STUDIES

Case 5.1   Equal Is Equal, or Is It?

Rosemary Manuel and Henry Summers worked as custodians at Wymore High School. Rosemary was in her first year as an employee of the Wymore school district, and Henry had served in the high school for four years. Both employees worked eight hours each day but one shift was from 6:00 a.m. to 2:00 p.m. and the other from 2:00 p.m. to

10:00 p.m. According to the school principal, the early work schedule and late work schedule was to change every six weeks; one custodian would work the early schedule for six weeks and then work the late schedule for the next six weeks.

Mathew Omar, the school principal, had filed three requests for additional custodial help for the high school but the reason given for the denial of the requests centered on a formula involving square footage of the school building, and Wymore did not qualify for more custodial help under the current policy.

On more than one occasion, Principal Omar had received notes from teachers that their rooms had not been cleaned satisfactorily: floors were dirty, waste baskets had not been emptied, desks had not been lined properly, chalkboards had not been erased and cleaned, and so forth. Principal Omar's most recent note was received from the new custodian Rosemary Manuel. Manuel complained that she was having to work overtime on both schedules since her service rooms included classes where art, home economics, chemistry, and industrial arts were taught. She also was scheduled for cleaning the four restrooms in the high school.

As Manuel stated, "the activities in the majority of my assigned rooms are especially messy and far more difficult to clean. Spilled paint in the art room, chemicals and instructional materials in the chemistry room, and food spills, dirty dishes, and sink, stove, and worktables in the home-economic rooms pose special cleaning energy and time. The industrial arts shops are especially messy."

Principal Omar did speak to custodian Summers about the scheduling situation. Summers's response was rather brief. He said that "work arrangements have been based on the factor of square footage ever since I have been at Wymore High. In my view, equal is equal. Anyway, Manuel hasn't seemed too happy at any time this year."

Principal Omar sent a note to Rosemary Manuel explaining that he had received her note of concern and that he would be back to her soon.

Case Study Follow-Up

Assume the role of Principal Omar and follow up with custodian Manuel and Summers administratively as you would do in practice. Avoid "resolving" the issues within the scenario by stating that you would seek more information or would meet with the two custodians and work things out. Although you might choose to do these two things, focus specifically on your thoughts about administrative leadership, problem solving, and fair and equitable treatment of employees. If you would plan to meet with the school district's HR director on this matter, do so with some ideas of your own regarding the problem and possible resolutions.

REFERENCES

Boyd County Public School District (2001, January 1). *Classified job descriptions.* Ashland, KY: Author.

Drucker, P.F. (2004). What makes an effective executive? *Harvard Business Review: Communication.* From the Web: https://hbr.org/2004/06/what-makes-an-effective-executive

Heathfield, S.M. (2016, June 1). *Performance management process checklist.* From the web: http://humanresources.about.com/od/glossary/p/g/perform_mgmt.htm

Lunenburg, F.C., & Ornstein, A.C. (2004). *Educational administration: Concepts and practices* (4th ed.). Belmont, CA: Wadsworth Thompson Learning.

Management Mentors (2016, May 30). *Business mentoring matters: How do the "100 best companies to Work for" attract top talent?* From the web: http://www.management_mentors.com/

Norton, M.S. (2008). *Human resources administration for educational leaders.* Thousand Oaks, CA: Sage.

Norton, M. S. (2016). *The legal world of the school principal: What leaders need to know about school law.* Lanham, MD: Rowman & Littlefield.

Pitt County Board of Education of Greenville, NC (2015, February 2). *Classified personnel: Suspension and dismissal.* Policy 7.208. Greenville, NC: Author.

State Civil Service, Louisiana (2013–14). *Report on turnover rates for non-temporary classified employees.* Prepared for the Joint Legislative Committee on the Budget, Shannon S. Templet, Civil Service Director, Louisiana State University.

Glossary

Action Distortion: The subject knows that he or she understood the message correctly but was reluctant to be different from an incorrect opinion of the majority.

Administration Regulation: A statement regarding how a policy is to be achieved. It answers the question of "How to do?" Administrative regulations commonly are determined by the school superintendent in cooperation with the school personnel.

Andragogy: The methods or techniques used to teach adults.

Application Screening: The evaluation and assessment of applications for the purpose of determining those persons who are to be placed in the applicant pool.

Change Management: Change management refers to any approach to transitioning individuals, teams, and organizations using methods intended to redirect the use of resources, business processes, budget allocations, or other modes of operation that significantly reshape the school district or school.

Classified/Support Personnel: School district employees who hold positions not requiring certification.

Competencies: The specific knowledge, skills, and abilities required for accomplishing a task.

Competency-Based Performance: A concept that serves to identify the primary tasks, competencies, and indicators of competency in relation to an employee's work requirements/purposes.

Designing Activity: Centers on creating plans of action that are focused on specific goals and objectives. It serves the human resources function in establishing strategies for implementation.

Double-Loop Learning: The learning process whereby the question of whether the operating norms in place are appropriate for the situation and the possibility that the school organization could self-adjust by determining the appropriate norms for the situation at hand are addressed.

Elite Power Structure: A power structure dominated by only 1% to 2% of the population.

Employee Engagement: A measure of school system health that serves as a key window into the potential future issues and workers' support for change.

Employee Mishandling: A term used in some cases to underscore inhuman resources (IR) rather than human resources (HR) within the personnel function.

Employee Orientation Guide: A resource handbook that sets forth the informational services and procedures for employees new to the school and/or school district.

Employment Assistance Program: School district program activities that serve troubled employees in many ways. The emphasis is on providing assistance to the worker in finding solutions and needed treatment that can best counsel and direct the worker in relation to the problem at hand while protecting the worth and dignity of the troubled employee.

Environmental Scanning: The possession and utilization of information about occasions, patterns, trends, opportunities, threats, and relationships within the school district's internal and external environments.

Evolutionary Changes: The continuous redesigning of the major processes of the human resources function.

Exit Interview: A human resources strategy used to collect information/data relative to an employee who is voluntarily leaving the school system. The interview might be completed in a face-to-face setting or by use of a written form that asks questions about the employee's work experiences and future plans.

External Scanning: Focuses on the strengths and weaknesses of the school system that support or inhibit the gaining of the district's full potential.

Facilitated Group Mentoring: Involves a group of teachers or other school employees who come together to achieve a specific learning goal.

Factional/Competitive Power Structure: Power is diffused among the members of the school community and, in turn, among the members of the school board. Depending on the issue at hand, the majority faction usually wins.

Forecasting: Looking toward the future and determining, evaluating, and assessing probabilities.

Formative Performance Evaluation: Focuses on purposes related to performance improvement and establishing the employee's individual development plan.

Group Mentoring: A strategy for mentoring groups of mentees as opposed to the common one-on-one mentoring strategy.

Indicators of Competency: The expected outcomes, products, and overt behaviors demonstrated by an individual employee.

Inert Power Structure: Inert or latent power structures commonly depend on the status quo. The school board generally depends on the school superintendent to make recommendations for its approval.

Integration: Using all available resources and opinions in a cooperative way to reach the best decision on a matter or the resolution of a problem facing members of the organization; when two parties are brought together for sharing their ideas on a matter based upon the facts of the case.

Internal Scanning: Focuses on the strengths and weaknesses within the organization that support or inhibit the district's full potential.

Job Families: The major position classifications/headings within the support staff under which various job graded positions exist.

Job Grading: The process of determining the value of jobs within a job family by considering the knowledge/skill levels required, levels of supervision given, nature of position responsibilities, and other factors related to the specific job.

Judgment Distortion: Occurs when the person believes that he or she interpreted the message incorrectly and the majority did not do so.

Long Interview: A technique of interviewing that uses strategies and activities to assess the candidate's strengths and weaknesses over a "lengthy" interview that includes morning and afternoon sessions, touring of school facilities, and meeting of members of the school personnel and community environment.

Markovian Analysis: An effective procedure for forecasting employee supply.

Organizational Climate: The collective personality of the school, school district, or school community characterized by the social and professional interactions within them.

Organizational Culture: The set of important assumptions, beliefs, values, and attitudes that members of the school, school district, or school community share.

Organizational Development: A body of knowledge and practice that enhances organizational performance and individual development by increasing alignment among various systems within the overall school system.

Organizing: The activity of using a systematic approach to the changes that are inevitable in the ongoing work of the human resources function; a systematic approach to decision making.

Pedagogy: The methods or techniques used to teach children.

Peer-Group Mentoring: Puts together a group of school/school district members with similar interests and needs to discuss issues and problems that are being encountered by the members.

Perception Distortion: Occurs when the person is not fully aware that he or she has misread or misinterpreted a message.

Performance Evaluation: The implementation of a variety of activities for the purpose of determining the employee's effectiveness in the respective position. Classroom performance evaluations, 360-degree evaluations, self-evaluations, performance evaluations, walk-through classroom visits, and other forms of determining an employee's work performance are in practice.

Performance Interview: Provides an opportunity to observe the candidate relative to the knowledge of the subject at hand, confidence and poise, oral communication, and instructional methods.

Performance Management: The process of creating a work environment in which employees are enabled to perform to the best of their abilities.

Planning: Planning is a strategic process that ties closely to change management. It is the foundational process by which the school board and administration evaluate and assess the effectiveness of personnel who must perform the required tasks that are needed to achieve the school district goals and objectives.

Pluralistic Power Structure: A power structure that is more open, and consensus is reached through discussion and diplomacy.

Position/Job Analysis: A scientific, comprehensive analysis of a job that includes its constituent parts and its internal and external conditions.

Position/Job Description: A statement that includes the guiding purposes of a position, the position's qualifications, supervision given and received, major position responsibilities, and other position requirements and responsibilities. Legally considered as an extension of the employee's employment contract.

Post-employment Orientation: Focuses on providing for effective and efficient transition of personnel into specific roles, including the work environment, personal assistance relative to material and supply sources for instruction, student information, disciplinary practices, student grading procedures, and the initiation of mentoring services.

Power Structure Analysis: The focus in general with the distribution of social power among groups in the school community which influences decision and decision making and how these groups and individuals work together to get things done.

Pre-employment Orientation: Those activities provided during the period between the initial contact with the school district and the time the candidate assumes an assignment in the school system.

Quality of Hire: The combination of calculating employee job performance, productivity, and job retention to determine the effectiveness of the school district's hiring procedures.

Range Figure: The figure assigned to a specific job after the process of job grading has been completed.

Recognition Analytics: Facilitating effective communication and fostering feedback loops in the school system by promoting cooperative bonds of recognition among employees in the school system.

Recruitment Organization: Centers on providing guidelines for implementing the recruitment process.

Re-recruitment: The extended efforts of the HR director and others to retain effective personnel in the school or school system. Also termed *strategic staffing*.

Reverse Mentoring: Typified by having a younger, more junior employee serve as the mentor for a senior, more experienced member of the organization.

Revolutionary*Changes*: Major changes in the fundamental processes of the human resources function.

School Policy: A school board statement that sets forth the goals and objectives of the personnel function and answers the question of "What to do?" A policy requires the approval of the board of education.

Single-Loop Learning: A condition is sensed, monitored, and scanned for current norm status, current norms are compared with operating norms, and the processes to make corrections to the appropriate norms are put into action.

Staff Orientation: The comprehensive complex of activities designed to gain congruency between institutional objectives and position needs.

Stay Interview: An interview completed periodically to learn what it will or would take for an employee to stay with the school system.

Strategizing: Centers on the activities required to reach desired goals and objectives. Strategizing serves the purpose of answering the question of what kind of strategy is the school district using for addressing ongoing change.

Structured Interview: Uses a series of prepared questions accompanied by specific *look-fors* to assess characteristics such as mission, empathy, listening, individualized instruction, focus, and innovation.

Subject Area Interview: Interview designed to gather information especially related to the position opening in question. Centers on content areas of preparation, knowledge, and skills related to the position and other affective characteristics of importance to effectiveness in the position.

Summative Performance Evaluation: Focuses on employment continuation, dismissal, and decisions relative to merit pay and job grade advancement.

System Efficiency: The school district's general management skills implemented for the purpose of keeping abreast of the organization's achievements toward stated goals and the critical need to meet ongoing human resources management challenges.

Task: A primary responsibility, requirement, or assignment of an employee's role/position.

Teacher Perceiver: Interview strategy that uses certain questions over and over in differing contexts. A scenario commonly is set forth whereby the employee candidate must describe what he or she would do on a matter at hand.

Trust: The concept of a person's willingness to be vulnerable to another person on the basis of confidence that the latter person is benevolent, reliable, competent, honest, and open (Hoy & Tschannen-Moran, *Journal of School Leadership*, 1999, 9, 184–208).

Vacancy Analysis: Focuses on determining employee movements over both short-range and long-range time periods.

Yield Ratios: The mathematical calculations used to determine the status of human resources processes in recruiting, hiring, and retention practices. (For example, seventy-five applications were received for classified positions in the school system, and fifty-six applicants were approved for the applicant pool; the yield ratio is 74.7%.)

About the Author

M. Scott Norton is a former public school mathematics teacher, coordinator of curriculum, assistant superintendent, and superintendent of schools. He served as Professor and Vice Chair of the Department of Educational Administration and Supervision at the University of Nebraska, Lincoln, later becoming Professor and Chair of the Department of Educational Administration and Policy Studies at Arizona State University, where he is currently Professor Emeritus. His primary graduate research and instruction areas include classes in human resources administration, the school superintendency, the school principalship, educational leadership, curriculum/instruction, the assistant school principalship, research methods, and competency-based administration.

Dr. Norton is the author and/or coauthor of college textbooks in the areas of the school superintendency, competency-based leadership, the principal as a student advocate, the school principal as a learning leader, great teachers, the legal world of the school principal, the assistant school principal, curriculum and supervision, and administrative management. He has published widely in national journals in such areas as teacher retention, teacher load, retention of quality school principals, organizational climate, classified personnel in schools, employee assistance programs, distance education, gifted student programs, and student retention. Four other books authored by Dr. Norton and published by Rowman & Littlefield are *The Principal as a Learning Leader: Motivating Students by Emphasizing Achievement*; *Competency-Based Leadership: A Guide for High Performance in the Role of the School Principal*; *Teachers with the Magic: Great Teachers Change Students' Lives*; and *The Legal World of the School Principal*. He is the coauthor of *Resources Allocation: Managing Money and People*. Two other books, *The School Principal as a Human Resources*

Leader and *The Assistant Principal's Guide: New Strategies for New Responsibilities*, were published in 2015.

Dr. Norton has received several state and national awards honoring his services and contributions to the field of educational administration from such organizations as the American Association of School Administrators, the University Council for Educational Administration, the Arizona Administrators Association, the Arizona Educational Research Association, Arizona State University College of Education (Dean's Award for excellence in service to the field), President of the ASU College of Education Faculty Association, and the Arizona Information Service (the distinguished service award). Most recently, Dr. Norton received a research grant from the Emeritus College at Arizona State University. The results of this research were reported in the aforementioned book, *The Legal World of the School Principal.*

Dr. Norton's state and national leadership positions have included service as Executive Director of the Nebraska Association of School Administrators, a member of the Board of Directors for the Nebraska Congress of Parents and Teachers, President of the Nebraska Council of Teachers of Mathematics, President of the Arizona School Administrators Higher Education Division, member of the Arizona School Administrators Board of Directors, Staff Associate of the University Council for School Administrators, Treasurer of the University Council for School Administrators, Nebraska State Representative for the National Association of Secondary School Principals, and member of the Board of Editors for the American Association of School Public Relations.

CPSIA information can be obtained
at www.ICGtesting.com
Printed in the USA
BVOW08*0042200317

478719BV00001B/2/P